The Holocaust Scream

Rachel Rosenberg Nazi Concentration Camp Survivor The Holocaust And That Scream

Rachel Rosenberg
With Robert Urban M.D.

The Holocaust Scream

Rachel Rosenberg

Nazi Concentration Camp Survivor

The Holocaust and That Scream

Table of Contents

Introduction – Rachel's True Story

Yes, there was a time, a place, a scream – The Holocaust Scream. A scream so penetrating that for Rachel Rosenberg, Jewish survivor of 4 concentration camps; it became the central point of her painful memories.

That Scream was her biggest hurt.

As a 14-year-old, Rachel was thrust into cruelty, destruction and death. She had to use her instincts, drive and cunning for survival under terrible conditions.

Death was all around. Hope was cruel. While in the camps, Rachel found ways to beat the odds and survive. She found a way to hide! How is that possible?

Rachel's story has some close parallels with Anne Frank's tragic experience. Both girls were teenagers, experienced fleeting young love, were blunt, admittedly naive and chronicler-victims of the Holocaust.

Anne Frank speaks through her diary. Fortunately, we have Rachel speaking for herself. Like Anne Frank, Rachel is refreshingly open, sensitive and honest. Rachel is a good storyteller.

Rachel made a difference for others. The ravages of the Nazi Holocaust did not end when the camp gates were forced open. Rachel had to endure even more hardship.

Rachel had to reconnect to all those things that we take for granted. It wasn't easy. Rachel had to take charge in order to get through the post-war turmoil. Rachel became a beacon offering help to many in need.

Determined to make the most of her situation, Rachel and her husband Carl became an American success story. Find out what Rachel did to reconnect with her strange new world after World War 2.

Rachel and her husband Carl were interviewed by movie director Steven Spielberg. Some of her concentration camp and ghetto experiences served as background for the movie, "Schindler's List."

Then there were those personal encounters with Nazis while in Omaha. Read about a mugging with the knife at the throat during a wrestling encounter with the much larger perpetrator.

Rachel has a "leading lady persona." Find out what that is.

Through a combination of narrative and dialogue, Rachel reveals a kaleidoscope of unfolding images and feelings. Each chapter of "The Holocaust Scream" is a vivid story. One sharp image and experience follows the other. "And then....," something else comes from Rachel's excellent memory.

I found a rhythm in Rachel's story. When I tried to combine her thoughts and feelings into larger paragraphs, immediately that rhythm or something was lost. I was trying to organize her story onto my life's template, not hers.

Watch for the rhythm. See if you agree about the rhythm.

Rachel has advice for those who find themselves in terrible circumstances.

Come in and meet Rachel. Findout about that terrible scream and the haunting aftermath of the Holocaust.

Warning:

Prepare to laugh, to cry.

Dedication

**To All Those Who Love Me, Who Loved
Me**

**And To Those Who Would Have Loved Me
– I Love You**

About the Authors and You

Rachel

You are about to learn who Rachel Rosenberg really is.

The Holocaust Scream chronicles Rachel's remarkable life from her teenage years through her ninth decade of life.

The Nazi camps robbed Rachel of a normal adolescence, most of her family, her ancestral environment and the strong spiritual support of her community. Rachel came out of the camps disconnected from most things we would consider normal.

After liberation from the Nazi camps, Rachel found purpose and direction in her life.

In time, Rachel and her family came to Omaha, Nebraska. There she encountered major barriers. Starting over, Rachel used her savvy, intelligence, determination and innate social skills to become an American success story.

Rachel has always wanted to tell her story, but held back. Her experiences were just too painful.

Now, Rachel has opened up and is pleased that the world is listening to her story. All her friends are glad she is getting her story out.

When you read her book, you will feel yourself connecting to this very special person. Are you ready?

Robert Urban M.D.

Robert Urban is an orthopedic surgeon and one of Rachel's many friends. There is a photo of Rachel and RTU in the website chapter of this book.

And You, Dear Reader.

Together, let's make The Holocaust Scream a living breathing document. For that, Rachel and I need your help. At the end of the book there is a chapter entitled, Insights.

Here you can add insights about the Holocaust, revelations you received as you pondered Rachel's story of the Holocaust and its meaning for you. Rachel's story will stir things within you.

As you know, the ebook format allows us to make updates to The Holocaust Scream from time-to-time.

When we update, we will include the best insights from the website where they are also permanently recorded.

With your added insights, Rachel's story will grow and stay alive as will your connection to the Holocaust.

What better way to keep the story alive than record your insights? Please add them to the comment section on our website at: www.theholocaustscream.com.

Here is what you should do. Go to the website. Record your insight in the comment section. Please make your comments brief.

If you are recording a personal opinion, I will reference your insight by: Insight Comment(s) from NAME and comments from the personal communication.

Please do not submit copyrighted material. If there is a source for facts, we would need to have you include the name, date and title for your source.

Become part of the story and permanently connect to the Holocaust remembrance. Join us. Record your insights and stay connected.

Thank You for Reading My Book

Thank you for reading my book. Would you please give me a review? With your help, we can make my book even better.

Keep the memories alive. Tell someone you know about The Holocaust Scream.

Love,

Rachel

Being a Bird - A Poem
by Arielle Vin'y
Rachel's Grandniece

"Being a Bird"

I envy the birds.

Free, light-hearted, in flight

Soar on a whim, take off as they please

Singing songs of happiness and hope.

But no –

I am not a bird, nor butterfly, or beetle.

I am a Jew, in a concentration camp

Numbered, locked-up, starved

Placed here to die.

I cannot escape or do as I please.

If only I were a bird,

Then I would be free.

"The Holocaust Never Happened?"

My name is Robert Urban. Rachel calls me Tom. I helped Rachel Rosenberg write her remarkable story.

I refer to myself as RTU in the text.

RTU:

Rachel, what is your reaction when you hear someone say, "The Holocaust never happened"?

Rachel:

"The Holocaust never happened?"

I would be devastated. I would cry my heart out. What kind of person is he? I have living proof. I am a Holocaust survivor.

I have a number on my hand. I lost my whole family. I lost my beautiful mom. She was 38 years old, put into the gas chamber alive with her 8-year-old son, little Motel.

How could anyone in this world right now say that the Holocaust didn't happen? That is, that person must be a very sick unknowledgeable person.

And he should be ashamed of himself to come up with such a question.

Meet Rachel and view her response on video at:

www.theholocaustscream.com .

What Did Rachel Lose? - "From Milk and Honey" Childhood - Idyllic Village - Beautiful Family

(RTU - On May 18, 2007, Rachel was interviewed by a close friend and neighbor, Abe Sass, a clinical social worker.

The interview was placed on file in the StoryCorps Archive in the American Folklife Center at the Library of Congress.

Excerpts from that interview will be added throughout this book.

As English is a second language for Rachel, please allow us to present her answers in her own words with as little editing as possible.)

RTU:

Abe Sass took notice when she commented,

"The air smells so wonderful."

Rachel was standing on the lawn outside his home in Omaha. Abe was struck by the fact that no one had ever made that statement in his presence.

Abe thought that Rachel must have "stuff" inside her that made her so excited to feel the outdoors and fresh air.

Abe:

Where do you think you get that quality to feel that way about the fresh air?

Rachel:

Well, when I grew up at home, I always liked the outdoors. I always enjoyed the beauty of the trees.

When I was little, my father rented orchards, in the summer, when the school was out. He moved us to the country into a little house.

We lived there about four months each summer, outdoors, among apples, pears and all kinds of beautiful fruit. I do love the outdoors and enjoy life just being outside.

I do like the fresh air.

(Rachel's Father – Moishe Bojman (Boiman) circa 1920– The Only Image of Rachel's Lost Family Members)

Abe:

You mentioned your father, what was he like? What kind of person was he?

Rachel:

My father was a cattle buyer at his profession. He was a wonderful father (and) good husband.

Abe:

How do you know he was such a good husband? He was your father.

Rachel:

Because I never heard him fight or have difficulties at home. I never heard that. He was a very kind person.

You know, at home, we didn't have any cars. He brought his cattles by hand.

When he would come home, he would put a piece of candy or chocolate under my pillow. Just for me. I never talked about this before.

He was a wonderful man. When Hitler came in, he was hidden in a barn. At night, I was a child. I took food to him.

I lost my father during the war. He was a wonderful man. He was 42 years old. His name was Moishe (Morris).

They killed him. All (many of) our children are named after my father. (Referring to her son Morris and several nephews.)

Mom was a beautiful lady. She was a good mom. Her name was Rose.

In the last day, I saw her, she baked her own bread. I saw her with a bag of flour on her back shoulders.

We were six kids. We had a wonderful home. We had from *milk and honey*. It was beautiful. I was a happy child.

I went to school. I was full of life. I didn't know from this.

I had cousins, grandparents from both sides. They all lived in the same area. They all lived in the same little town of Wolanow.

Abe:

What did the town look like?

Rachel:

It was maybe smaller than Lincoln (Nebraska). It was not developed like Lincoln is. I don't think we had electric lights. I don't think we had water in our homes.

Abe:

Really? So how did you get water?

Rachel:

From a well, in buckets. A special man, called a sholom (sp?), brought water in from outside the town. Isn't that something?

Abe (softly):

Yes. It is.

Rachel:

I was maybe 10 years old, but I didn't know any better. We had freedom. We had everything.

Then, everything was destroyed. Hitler came in 1939 and we were taken to the camps. We were all separated.

Abe:

Did you have friends, best friends, while you were growing up?

Rachel:

Yes. I did.

Abe:

What was that like?

Rachel:

It was a happy time. It was a happy time. I went to school, came home, did our homework. It was happy. It was nice. It was a very small time.

We were happy (with) whatever we had.

Abe:

Did you like school?

Rachel:

Yes. Yes, I did. I think I had only about the sixth grade and then the war broke out.

Abe:

Do you remember when you were a kid? What were some of the things you liked to do just for fun?

Rachel:

Goin' in the fields. That's a good question. I went with my mother. We picked potatoes and beans.

My favorite was going in the fields and picking blue flowers. What do you call those flowers? I don't know.

A blue little flower. That was my, my love. Just going into the weeds, the corn, picking those blue flowers and making bracelets.

You love me, you love me not. We made them and put them around our foreheads. That was, the outdoors, was my passion.

Abe:

It still is, it sounds like, because you love to garden.

Rachel:

Yes.

Abe:

So, did you find yourself doing this with friends or just with your mom?

Rachel:

Not with friends, with my mom.

Abe:

That's a very sweet memory. What did she look like?

Rachel:

My mom was beautiful, just like I am.

Abe (laughing softly):

Rachel:

My mother was a beautiful... She had black beautiful long hair. She had her mother and father there. It was a family.

Abe:

So, your grandparents lived with you also?

Rachel:

No. No. They lived in a different... in that little small town. Friday night was beautiful with baked stuff, with a table cloth, with candles.

My father was a religious man. He went to the synagogue. When he came home, he always brought somebody to our table. Somebody who did not have.

He was at our table. We had the best food and all the children sat together.

Abe:

And this was every Friday night? How did he find somebody to bring home on a Friday night? Would he just see somebody?

Rachel:

There was somebody in the synagogue who didn't have a home, was going through the little town and couldn't go home for the Shabbat (Friday night – Saturday weekly Jewish Sabbath.)

My father always had one or two people for ... that was a mitzvah. It was a good deed. I remember that.

Why Rachel Never Forgot Her First Love

Abe:

Did you have any boyfriends when you were a kid?

Rachel:

Yes. I had a lot of boyfriends. But I didn't want anybody. Because everybody was picking at me; my hair, my eyes. I didn't know life.

I was afraid of men. No, I didn't have a boy – not really. I was young.

Abe:

When you were growing up, you mentioned there were boyfriends who liked you, but you didn't (like any of them). How did you eventually meet your husband?

Rachel:

I am going to tell you about a boyfriend. I am going to go back.

Abe:

Ah.

Rachel:

During the war, people came from big cities to our little city to avoid the horror, but it wasn't so.

My father was a butcher. He had a butcher shop. A very wealthy family from Lodz (Poland) came in. They had a son. They had a couple sons.

But one son, he was so handsome. He was so good. He kinda fell in love with me. That's true.

'Til today, I still have dreams of him. If he would live through the war, I know he would find me.

He did not want to go to the concentration camp. He was hiding among the facilities in our town, among the gentiles.

One day, somebody tipped them. They said he was Jewish.

They took him out and killed him. But, I did have a boyfriend who loved me.

I did not understand what that (boyfriend) means. He brought me some clothes. He brought me shoes. But, then I didn't understand.

He went to a different town, because they were looking for him.

Abe:

Who was looking for him?

Rachel:

The police.

Abe:

So, you mean the local police?

Rachel:

The Germans, the SS (fanatical Hitler devotees/soldiers). Then, he came at night to see me. You know, they made a ghetto. May I talk about this?

Abe:

You may talk about whatever you want.

Rachel:

All the Jews had to live in one corner of the city (the Wolanow ghetto). We had about 5 families living in our home.

Me and my mom with the children lived in the attic.

I now remember when he (young Morris-from-Lodz) came and crawled up into the attic. He brought me some things.

I remember like it was today. So, I did have a boyfriend.

Abe:

What was his name?

Rachel:

Morris.

Abe:

Ah-hah. And you're not sure what happened to him?

Rachel:

Yes. They shot him. They killed him. But, a few of his family lived through the war in concentration camps. I don't know how many. Maybe two or three survived.

(Pause - Interview with Abe Sass – to be resumed later)

(RTU - I recently asked Rachel if she had more memories of her young love from Lodz, Poland.)

RTU:

Rachel, when you were interviewed by your friend Abe Sass, you mentioned you grew fond of a young boy and he grew fond of you.

Can you tell us a little more about that time in your life?

Rachel:

Okay, that was Wolanow (ghetto) and I was a 14-year-old shy little girl. But, I happened to be very beautiful.

There was a family and their name was Schnatovsky (sp?). They came from a bigger town, Lodz, to escape to our little Wolanow.

But, that was wrong. Wolanow was hit very hard by the Nazis. So anyway, me and my mom, and I don't know, all the children, we had three boys, slept in the attic.

I slept in the attic with my mom.

And then one day, it was night. Morris came to see me. He brought me some clothes. He brought me some patent leather shoes and gave it to me.

And so, I happened to like him very much.

At that time, we were in the ghetto. We needed meat. My father was a cattle buyer.

So, they brought in cattles at night when the Germans were away. They brought cattle and we had a house.

On the same ground, a little bit farther, we had a butcher shop. They took in the cows at night, when it was quiet, with a shochet (kosher ritual butcher).

And, they killed the animals in the kosher style.

Morris (from Lodz) helped my father and mother, my family, when they came to Wolanow. And I happened to love him, fell in love with him.

Then, he ran away some place. I didn't see him.

31

One time, at night, he came up to see me. Then, we were all going to the concentration camp.

RTU (interrupting):

Now wait a minute. Can I ask you.....?

Rachel:

He didn't want to go.

RTU:

When he came to see you, he was in danger. Was he not?

Rachel:

He was in very much danger. He came at night.

RTU:

So they were looking for him?

Rachel:

They were looking for him. And then, he left at night.

RTU:

So, he came to see you at the risk of his life?

Rachel:

Right.

RTU:

Do you know what he wanted to do? Do you remember what he said to you?

Rachel:

Well, I think what he wanted to do is take me from my family, to go with him. I cried and told my mom, "No. I am not going no place."

So, then he left. Then, he came every night. He came to visit.

RTU:

For how long?

Rachel:

For maybe a week, two weeks.

RTU:

Did he still want to take you?

Rachel:

So I told him, "I'm not going." But, he brought some clothes, some special foods and he talked to me.

He helped my mom and dad. He helped them get the butcher shop ready for the fresh meat.

One day, they took us all out. He (Morris) didn't want to go to the concentration camp. So, he went to a big, big farm called Szalkev (sp?). He worked there for a little bit.

I went to the Szalkev Concentration Camp, which was in the middle of the Szalkev farm where Morris (from Lodz) worked among the Gentiles.

Then, I heard that somebody tipped. I don't know if he had false papers and that he's not a Jew. He was kinda of a blond and did not look Jewish.

They tipped the Germans that he was a Jewish boy and he was shot. He was killed.

I never saw him again.

But, (for) a long, long time I had nightmares of him. I knew that after the war, that if he (Morris) ever lived through the war, no matter where he would be, he would look me up.

But, then I heard he was shot on that farm.

RTU:

Do you remember the last time you saw him?

Rachel:

Yes. The last time I saw him, he brought me food. He talked to me and kinda looked at me.

He took me around and he told me how beautiful I am and how much he loved me. And I loved him.

RTU:

Did you tell him you loved him?

Rachel:

I did tell him. But in the middle of the night, he left to his place.

RTU:

Did he say he was going to come back to you?

Rachel:

He said he might come back, but he never did.

RTU:

Do you know the story of Romeo and Juliet?

Rachel:

No. I do not.

RTU (softly):

Okay. Well, you are Juliet in the story.

Rachel:

Really?

RTU:

His last...Yes...

Rachel:

I loved him and I had nightmares from him. Lately, I didn't. For a long, long time I had nightmares, that he came in my dreams a lot.

RTU:

Did he ever talk to you in your dreams?

Rachel:

Yeah, he talked to me, but I don't remember what. But then he was very handsome, tall and gorgeous, a gorgeous young man.

RTU:

Do you have any other things to add? How old was he?

Rachel:

"Maybe in the twenties. Twenty-five?"

RTU:

....Getting back to Morris-from-Lodz. Did you ever hold hands or anything like that?

Rachel:

Yes. We walked. We held hands.

RTU:

Did you ever kiss?

Rachel:

I don't remember if we kissed or not. That I don't remember. But, I loved him with all my might as a 14-year-old.

Because he was very, very good to me. And he really loved me. But, it was not meant to be. He didn't live through the war.

RTU:

But, your love lasted, in a way, forever.

Rachel:

Yes, my love.

RTU:

Talking about him, you still love him.

Rachel:

I still love him.

RTU (softly):

In your way. huh?

Rachel:

Yep, he was one-of-a-kind, boy in the world.

RTU:

Thank you, Rachel, for sharing that.

(RTU – This is a poignant story of young love sprouting with all its potential. I couldn't help but think of the Shakespeare's tragedy, "Romeo and Juliet," the star-crossed lovers.

Young Morris-from-Lodz did risk his life to see Rachel. It was a risk he was willing to take over and over. She was worth it, the power of young love.

I find this story emotionally powerful every time I read it. There is raw simplicity, Young Love trying to assert itself even in the face of Death.

We would like to know what you think? You can comment at:

www.theholocaustscream.com

(End of follow-up interview with RTU)

When Did the Predators Come? The Holocaust Begins

(RTU - The Germans invaded Poland on September 1, 1939. Hitler and his Nazis made a false accusation that Poland had attacked an isolated border station between the two countries.

The other European powers had made Poland a line in the sand. There was to be no more tolerance of Germany's aggression.

When Germany crossed the Polish border, England and France immediately declared war on Germany. World War 2 was officially underway.

In the United States, there was a strong pacifist movement. The pacifists did not want to go down the same road that had taken the United States into World War 1.

Staying out of European affairs was the best course for these pacifists and other pragmatists.

I had occasion to meet a former president of a college pacifist group. She told me the group was very large and active in anti-war issues.

I asked her what happened to the pacifist group. She said, "After Pearl Harbor, there were no pacifists."

Later, Rachel wonders where the United States was throughout the Holocaust. The United States was reluctant to get involved in European here-we-go-again affairs.

When the Japanese attacked Pearl Harbor in 1941, Germany unilaterally declared war on the United States. Germany and Japan had a mutual assistance pact.

The U.S. declared war on Germany a few days later. By the time the United States entered the two front war, Rachel had been in the camps for about 2 years.)

Rachel continues:

When I was 14, the Germans came. There did not seem to be a reason for their coming, but there they were.

When the war broke out, I was in a little town in Poland called Wolanow. I don't remember Wolanow so much by size, but how peaceful it was.

Wolanow was a religious town in that there were many churches and synagogues sprinkled throughout the town.

Every block had a church. There was no separate Jewish section. Otherwise, in the 1930s, Wolanow was a quiet farming village in central Poland.

I was born in Wolanow in the mid-20s. I believe I was born on August 1, 1926. I am not completely sure.

All the records from that time have been destroyed. As people gathered together, sometimes dates and times became fuzzy and confused.

We might not agree on the details. That is why I am not completely sure of my birthday.

People say that you cannot take away a person's birthday. In a way, the Germans were able to take mine.

We had a wonderful beautiful home. Everyone was happy all the time, or so it seemed to me. I was one of six children. My parents were Moishe (Morris) and Rose Bojman (Boiman).

I had two sisters. Mania was four years older, while Bluma was three years younger. We had 3 brothers, Motel, Jacob and the oldest, Aaron.

My father was a cattle buyer. My mother was a seamstress. My father was handsome and my mother was beautiful.

In those days, girls were expensive. The family had to pay a lot of money in the form of a naden or dowry.

Mania, my older sister, married before the outbreak of the war. My father had to pay a large dowry to get her a man.

(RTU - As was the custom and socially acceptable at the time, money was paid from the bride's family to the groom's family as part of the typical marriage arrangements.)

Mania became separated from her husband when the Germans came. Her husband's name was Choski Cooper.

When I was in my first camp, Choski was on his way to see me when he was captured and shot. I do not know the details or why he was coming to see me.

My father used to tell me that I was beautiful and, as a result, I wouldn't cost him anything. This made me feel good. I always had a sense that I was pretty.

I didn't know about sex in any way. I didn't know where babies came from. I actually thought that if a man touched a woman, she would become pregnant.

I would not let boys get close enough to touch me. I remember a boy in my village wanting to get close to me. He chased me and I ran. I hid under some bushes, but he did not find me.

Later in the camps, I tried with all my efforts to avoid being touched by a German soldier.

I still had that fear that babies came from being touched by a man. I didn't know better at the time.

I loved my mother with all my life. I did not like her food for whatever reason. She was a good cook. I was spoiled and took advantage of it.

My parents arranged for a neighbor to fix my meals. I would eat with the neighbors. Now that I am an adult, this seems very strange to me.

Generally, I had a very happy childhood. One of my fondest memories was an orchard which my father rented every summer.

We children had access to the orchard all summer long. We stayed in a farmhouse on the property.

My father peddled the fruit in the city. We harvested the fruit for 3 months.

When the Germans came, that all changed.

The first thing the Germans did was bomb the city. I was in the middle of a field with my brother Jacob.

We did not get hurt, but a lot of people got hurt and killed. I saw a lot of dead bodies.

My mom took the linens off the bed to help the hurt. There were a lot of hurt people.

The Germans came in on green motorcycles with three Germans on each motorcycle.

I was fourteen and hid with other children in the houses. We were afraid of the Germans. We knew there was a war.

But, I had no idea the Germans were going to destroy us, that they were going to kill us.

The Wolanow Ghetto - Mom and My Youngest Brother, Motel, Are Murdered

Rachel:

After the Germans came, in a few days, they made a ghetto.

One day, on Yom Kippur, the Day of Atonement, Germans surrounded the town and separated the population according to age and sex.

I never was in the presence of my whole family again.

Our house was in the one section of Wolanow, which became the ghetto. There were four or five families totaling 15 to 20 people in our house.

We had two bathrooms. Our home had a basement and upstairs attic. People slept on the top floor. I slept in our attic with my mom.

I remember screaming at night as I slept with my mom. My dream was of my mother being taken away. We did not know what was waiting for us.

The Germans built concentration camps right away. At first, the Germans held gypsies and others in these camps.

But, the Germans killed them all just before we were sent to the camps. The Germans had to make room for us.

In Wolanow (town), the first thing the Germans did was to take out all the doctors, lawyers, educators, business people, and the rich people.

They kept them about three days in a shelter. After that, they were taken into a small forest and killed one-by-one.

As kids, we asked around about who was killed. Someone told us that my father was not among the dead. The dead bodies were left until someone dug a grave for each of them.

I wondered about my father. When the Germans rounded up the others, he had sneaked off to a barn.

Our city was a farm city. We had cattle as did many others.

At night, on my own, I begin to search for him as I was told he was not in the group that had been killed.

I went to one barn after another calling, "Dad. Dad."

In the third barn, I found my father. He was hiding among the hay. When I saw him, he was not shaved, shaking and hungry.

His hands were bloody. He told me the mice and rats came at night and ate his fingers.

I started to scream and he told me to stop. He did not want anyone to hear. I took him home.

I was the only one of my family who went out to help the others.

After a few days, the Germans came for him and took him to one of the camps. Later I learned that he became sick from typhus and couldn't walk.

He was shot in the camp (Buchenwald in Germany) four weeks before the war was over. Many people later reported to me that they saw him shot.

This was 1940, when my father was first taken. My father was 42 years old and a beautiful man when he went into the camp.

I was probably in Auschwitz with him at some time, but I never saw him. Men and women were always kept separate in the camps.

My father had survived Auschwitz and went to Buchenwald Camp near the end of the war. They made him walk and walk. It bothers me to this day.

He didn't even have a grave. I don't know if they buried him. He was a good man and never hurt anyone, but the Germans were brutal.

Where was the world? Where was the United States?

Where was anybody? It was a mass murder.

There was a time in Auschwitz when they took 1,400 people, including my future husband Carl's sister, Tova.

They were on a ship sailing around. No country would take them. Finally, somebody sank the ship.

(RTU - This is an intriguing story. On several occasions, Rachel has related this story to me.

Rachel is adamant, consistent and unwavering that some people were taken, during the war, from the land-locked Auschwitz Concentration Camp in Poland, placed on a boat, only to die in the end.

According to Rachel's recollection, the Germans took the people out of the Auschwitz camp. The boat was eventually sunk because, "No one would take them."

Rachel does not know any more details or how she came by this information.

(RTU - There is the well-documented story of the S.S. St. Louis. The S.S. St. Louis was a ship of German registry.

Prior to the outbreak of WW 2 by several months, the St. Louis sailed from Hamburg, Germany, to Cuba with 937 refugees fleeing Europe. 930 of the refugees were Jewish.

Upon arrival in the Havana, Cuba harbor, the 930 refugees learned that Cuba had recently changed its refugee laws.

As a result of a hastily contrived technicality and as a deliberate barrier, the refugees could not disembark as tourists or refugees.

There was an attempt to exhort the refugees. Most did not have money for the roughly $500 "bond."

Consequently, only a few were able to get off the ship in Havana.

President Roosevelt and other top American officials encouraged the Cuban government to admit the refugees from the S.S. St. Louis to no avail.

The S.S. St. Louis sailed for the United States, but was denied entry.

American naval vessels were sent to shadow the S.S. St. Louis while it was in American waters.

The Americans were concerned the Captain would run the ship aground and let the passengers enter the United States.

The Captain of the S.S. St. Louis, Captain Gustav Schroder, was a non-Jewish German citizen.

Captain Schroder later admitted that he considered running his boat aground off the coast of the United States.

He was prevented from grounding the S.S. St. Louis by the two American vessels which constantly and closely followed his boat.

Likewise, Canada denied the refugees safe landing.)

(S.S. St. Louis Captain Gustav Schroder negotiating landing permits for the refugees at Antwerp, Belgium docks 1939.)

(RTU continues) -

Captain Schroder insisted that his passengers be treated with dignity at all times.

With the start of World War 2 just six weeks away, Captain Schroder and several European governments negotiated the settlement of the refugees in non-German jurisdictions, e.g. England, France and Belgium.

Approximately 600 of the original 930 passengers of the S.S. St. Louis landed in continental Europe.

Many were captured and sent to German concentration camps during the war as the Nazi war machine swept over Europe.

Captain Schroder insisted he would not return the ship to Germany until all the passengers were landed in non-German jurisdictions. Landing permits were rationed.

No one country would take a large number of his passengers!

As we know, Captain Schroder was able to get the necessary permits with difficulty, but just in time for some of his passengers.

It is thought that about 300 of the original St. Louis Jewish refugees perished during the war.

The S.S. St. Louis survived the war. Captain Schroder received the Order of Merit from the

Federal Republic of Germany (Post-war German Government allied with the West).

In addition, Captain Gustav Schroder was post-humously named as one of the Righteous Among the Nations at the Yad Vashem Holocaust Memorial in Tel Aviv.

The S.S. St. Louis saga has lent fuel to the critical notion that western governments always knew more about what was happening to the Jews in Europe than they were willing to admit.

As we can see, Rachel's story could not be the story of the S.S. St. Louis. The number of passengers, the starting point, the timing and sinking are not the same.

Rachel's ship story needs to have its place and chance in history. Maybe, just maybe, there was another ship with 1400 doomed souls who sailed to their deaths, but not quite into oblivion.

Rachel may be the only voice who can speak for them!)

Rachel continues:

We were afraid of the Germans. I never talked to the Germans during my 6 years in the camps. No one knew what was going to happen.

I had 3 little brothers (Aaron 16, Jakob 9 and Motel 8). On my own, I went to the church where my father supplied their meat.

I asked the priest if they would keep those three boys. No one would know they were Jewish. He was afraid to take them.

If someone would tip the Germans, the whole family would be shot. This (shooting of sympathetic gentile families) was happening at the time.

I remember hearing about sympathetic families being shot.

There was a pregnant lady. She had her baby in a barn. After 2 days, she left the baby on a Gentile doorstep.

After the war, both Jewish parents came to the town and were able to reclaim the baby boy.

He was then six years of age. I do not know if it was easy or hard for them to get the boy back. I later met this boy, who became a successful businessman in Los Angeles. His name is Marty.

We did not know what was waiting for us. The Poles didn't do anything. The Poles stayed away. The Jews could not hide. No one talked about the situation. We didn't fight.

Just before I entered the camp, I wanted to gather my family. My mother had given me a golden coin. She said to use it to buy bread.

On my own, I used the coin to pay a Polish gentile to take me to the small town of Schelovitz (sp?).

My mom, my youngest brother, Motel, and her family were there. We went by horse and buggy and it took a while.

When I came to my mom's apartment, she was with my youngest brother. She said, "My child, I am going to cook you your favorite dish."

This was potatoes, noodles and onions.

I told my mom to pack a few things and come with me. She said she was too busy, but that she would join me in a day or two.

I went back to Wolanow. I was not happy. I went back to her to try again to get her to come with me. I had told her I could not live without her.

Mom gave me a package of clothes. The last time I went back for mom, her apartment was empty. She was gone.

There was never a next day. It was Yom Kippur, the Jewish Day of Atonement.

When she went to the synagogue, the Germans rounded up all the Jews and took them away. Mania and Bluma didn't go to the synagogue, they hid in the attic.

I began to search for my sisters. Mania had hidden in the barns when the Germans first came. Now there was no place for her to hide.

If she had been discovered, she would have been sent to the gas chambers for avoiding the round-up going to the Wolanow Ghetto.

I felt both Mania and mom would be better off with me in the ghetto.

When I found mom and Motel gone, I searched and found Mania (sister - survivor) and Bluma (other sister and survivor). Mania told me mom was gone.

I was so upset I fell to the groung. I had a nose bleed and felt very sick, because I didn't have my mother.

I brought Mania and Bluma back to the Wolanow ghetto. I found out about a week later my mom had been killed by gas in Treblinka.

She and my youngest brother, Motel, were together and upon arriving at Treblinka, they were sent directly to the gas chambers.

We began to understand what the Germans were doing.

Rachel:

After a while, they (the German SS) came in with dogs. They were beautifully dressed in their uniforms. I remember the skulls on their uniforms. It was terrifying.

I Leave Wolanow Ghetto - My Brother, Aaron, Is Shot

(Nazi SS Death Head Collar Insignia)

Rachel:

I remember my journey from Wolanow (town). It was a beautiful day. We were ordered to leave with just our clothing and no possessions.

We opened the door and walked out.

As I was leaving, I saw a cup and saucer which I had bought for my mom as a mother's day present. Mother's Day was a special day in Poland.

I turned back to get the cup and saucer. I grabbed the cup and saucer, but a German SS guard hit me and took the cup and saucer.

I was not sent to Wolanow Concentration Camp. Most of my family went there. I was sent to Szalkev Concentration Camp. I do not know how we came to be separated.

We all left for the first camps on the same day. We were loaded into separate trucks and when I got off the truck, my family was not with me.

While the rest of my family was still in Wolanow Concentration Camp, the Germans made death selections every couple of days.

They took out people to be killed. They took them for no reason.

Sometimes, it would be every other person in line. Sometimes, they would walk through the lines of people and make selections.

We knew the ones they chose were going to die. We were terrified.

Wolanow Camp did not have the barbed wire fences. It was possible to sneak out. One day, everyone felt that something bad was about to happen.

Mania and Bluma sneaked out and hid for a while in a barn.

My oldest brother, Aaron, was 16 years old. He hid in a barrel. He was taken out and shot during the assembly. The Germans kicked the barrel over and shot him.

My sister Bluma and other relatives witnessed the shooting. Bluma and Mania had come back into the camp.

My relatives went over to his dying body and hugged and kissed him. The blood was running from him. They knelt over him.

My father had given Aaron about 500 Polish dollars. Aaron had it on his person when he was shot. Bluma knew this.

She laid her body across his bleeding body and took the money from his clothes. She was covered in Aaron's blood.

I was in Szalkev Concentration Camp. Sometimes, we were taken out in the fields to do work. We had no contact with the Poles.

Just like in the Wolanow Camp, there was no barbed wire. Yes. I could leave, but there was no place to go.

In Szalkev Camp, we slept on benches like herring one-by-one. I was with my aunt, Tova, who had one of her children with her.

I don't remember his name. He was 2 years old. One of the male guards shot the child while Tova was holding him.

Only the male guards did the shooting while I was in the camps.

The women guards were more brutal than the male guards. The female guards pushed us and yelled at us all the time. The women guards were SS.

(RTU - The SS women were in elite Nazi paramilitary groups. SS is an abbreviation for Shutz or protection coupled with Staufel or staff (squadron).

The SS men rose early in the history of the Nazi party. They served as guards to protect the Nazis in their contentious formative years.

Over time, the SS units became elite and grew in numbers.

There were SS subgroups. SS units were organized in conquered countries. Austria had a large German-speaking population. Many Austrians joined the SS units.

There was a infamous Belgium Walloon Batallion of SS. As the 300 volunteers went to join the Germans in the east, they were romanticized by the Belgium press despite their dark deeds.

They had become national heroes. 20 came back.

Hitler demanded the SS be racially pure from the Nordic or Aryan perspective.

True to their purpose and special relationship with Hitler, the SS continued to search out and eliminate so-called enemies of Hitler long after the Nazi cause was lost.

The women SS belonged to the SS-Helferinnenkorps or "Women Helper Corps." These women volunteers joined the SS as auxiliaries.

These women had a lesser SS status. They did not participate in combat. Membership in the regular SS was forbidden to women.

The SS-Helferinnenkorps was used for administrative purposes providing personnel, clerks and female camp guards.

That is how these SS women came to be in front of Rachel.

Rachel continues:

Once a day, they cooked a soup in a massive kettle with food that was usually fed to animals. Kohlrabi?

Many times, I would be the server of the soup. I don't know why I was chosen. This was extra work for me.

I would serve the food as soon as we came in from working in the fields. Then we would go to our barracks.

As much as I could, I would try to give extra portions to people, especially people I knew. I never ran out of soup.

RTU:

Were you able to get more food because you were a server?

Rachel:

No. That was not possible.

RTU:

What did the other prisoners think when you gave extra portions to some?

Rachel:

No one knew. There was a line and the people back in the line didn't get to see what I was doing.

The guards didn't care. No one complained or made a noise about this.

RTU:

Why do think no one complained?

Rachel:

It was not safe to complain. Ever. You could be killed on the spot. We did not want to call attention to ourselves by making any noise.

RTU:

What about nightmares and screaming at night?

Rachel:

At night, the barracks were as quiet as can be. There were guards around. If you screamed or made any noise, that could be the end for you.

I remember giving extra food to my aunt Mimi from the town of Radem, (Poland). After the war, she would thank me many times for giving her that extra food.

The air was cold and we did not have much for covers.

Once in a blue moon they might give us a mildewed piece of bread. The Germans told us the mildewed bread contained penicillin and it was good for us.

(RTU: In 1928, Scotsman Alexander Fleming discovered the antibiotic, penicillin, by chance. Penicillin was the first antibiotic to kill bacteria.

Sulfa drugs had been discovered by a German, Gerhard Domagk, before penicillin. Sulfa drugs inhibited, but might not kill bacteria. Penicillin was the better antibiotic, a true wonder drug for the times.

The discovery and use of penicillin was a tipping point and game-changer with regard to the care of war wounds. The death and amputation rates from war wounds were dramatically lowered for the wounded with access to penicillin.

The guards, living in the sophisticated new world of penicillin, were mocking the prisoners. Penicillin is very dose sensitive. Any penicillin found on a piece of bread would be insignificant.

Rachel remembers the taunting and reference to penicillin. Penicillin was a big deal at the time.

Fleming and Domagk each received the Nobel Prize for their work.)

Rachel:

On one occasion, I remember one incident where a 5-year-old boy from Wolinow town fell into a boiling kettle of soup.

There was a walking platform above the soup and he just fell in. I did not see him fall, but I remember there was a lot of noise when he fell into the boiling soup kettle.

Everyone, even the guards, seemed concerned and rushed to help him. They were able to pull him out, but later he died.

I saw him after they pulled him out. It was sad. I knew his parents from Wolinow.

Whoever got sick was set aside for a day or two. If they did not get better, they were killed. There were no doctors. A few doctors were among the prisoners.

There was a girl in our barracks who got pregnant by a German soldier. She was 22, maybe 25. She wore a guard so they wouldn't see her stomach.

This only happened once in our barracks. This woman slept above me and had come from Warsaw. She had experience in a lot of things I knew nothing about.

I didn't know where babies come from.

The woman had been in the camp for more than 9 months. Had the Germans found out about the pregnancy, there would have been a terrible scandal.

We could all have been killed.

How she became pregnant, I do not know. There were male German guards, as well as male German administrators, who worked in the camp offices. Male and female prisoners didn't mix at any time.

These administrators were not in the SS.

After the baby was born, the women in the barracks took the baby at night and killed it. I did not witness this.

No one talked about the details. The others told me only that the baby had been killed.

(RTU – Hitler, and consequently the Nazis, were obsessed with racial purity. In 1920, Hitler published a 25 Point Program for the Nazi Party's open political agenda.

The 25 Point program included –

- A demand for Germanic racial purity – the Master Race

- Germany was destined to rule over all other inferior races - The Thousand-Year Reich

- Jews were a separate race and racial enemies of the German race.

- The fact that the Jews were a separate religious group was a minor consideration.

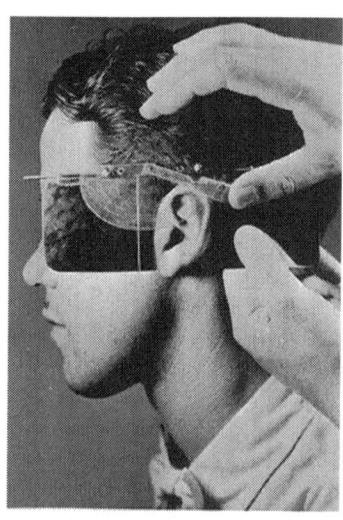

(Establishing racial descent by measuring an ear at the Kaiser Wilhelm Institute for Anthropology, Berlin – date unknown.)

Over time, Hitler and many Germans took up the mantle of racial purity and tried to establish biological markers indicating racial purity.

Many German citizens became obsessed with measuring. They measured every physical feature trying to identify the criteria for the purest of the Germanic race.

Many German citizens were fascinated by the meaning of their personal racial markers. There developed an informal racial purity pecking order built around the Nordic traits.

The ones who had the most traits were "the most pure Aryans."

For over a hundred years, some people were fascinated by the concept of a Master Race. Many Germans, especially the Nazis, believed that the Aryan people were descendents from the lost city of Atlantis.

To the Germans, these Aryans were more racially pure and superior to everyone else. Therefore, the Aryans should and could rule the world.

The Germans under Hitler chose themselves as the Master Race.

The Nazi's new world was to be better-off with Aryan leadership. The losers were people like Rachel and the other 80 million people estimated to have died as result of World War 2.

Fraternizing between Jews and Germans was prohibited and not tolerated. German soldiers having sex with Jews were accused of mixing impurities into the Master Race which was to be kept pure.

Soldiers could be sent to the dreaded Russian Front for raping a Jew. Purity, not morality, was an obsession and the most important issue.)[1]

Rachel continues:

As for leaders in the barracks, we had fellow Jewish prisoners (capos) who watched us and reported to the Germans. Carl's brother, Nathan, was a capo guard.

(RTU - Rachel had known Carl Rosenberg from her pre-war days in Wolanow. Carl and Rachel married after the war. Later she will discuss her relationship with Carl in more detail.)

One day Carl's brother went over a boundary and was caught. He was placed in a building and shot in a day or two.

He had to dig his own grave. I witnessed his killing.

Nathan was 24 years old and a beautiful young man.

I have no idea why they waited a day to kill him or why he had to dig his own grave. Maybe it had something to do with the fact that he was a guard of sorts who worked with the Germans.

In the Wolanow Camp administration office was a Jewish woman who tried to hide her identity. She had false papers.

In time, someone tipped the Germans that she was Jewish. The Germans killed her right away.

In the middle of the Szalkev Camp, there was a box to be used as a toilet. There was no soap or water. There were lice. I had them. So did everyone else.

I remember the lice crawling on me and biting me. I remember a lot of itching and scratching. I remember the lice being especially drawn to our armpits.

There was not much we could do, but pick the lice off each other.

We were kids. We were teenagers. We were scared.

In Szalkev Camp, I was with my middle brother, Jacob. I don't remember how he came to be with me.

After a year, he was taken away. After a couple more years, Jacob came back and was with me again for a while in Auschwitz.

(RTU - At one time, the Germans considered closing the Szalkev Concentration Camp. There was a very active typhus epidemic. The Germans wanted to eradicate the epidemic for their own protection.

The plan was in place. All the inmates in the camp would be killed. Carl, Rachel's future husband, found out about it. He convinced the Germans to leave the Szalkev Concentration Camp open.

Carl told the German soldiers that they would be sent to the collapsing Russian front if they weren't kept busy.

Eventually the Szalkev Camp was closed before the end of the war.)

Who am I? - Auschwitz - #15254 - The Camp Routine

(Entry Gate At Auschwitz)

Rachel:

In 1942, I was taken to Auschwitz. I stayed three years in Auschwitz. We were brought there by cattle cars.

There was a saying over the camp entry gate which said –

Arbeit Macht Frei (Work Makes You Free).

We immediately received a number by tattoo. They never used our names, just the numbers. My number is 15254 and I have it with me today.

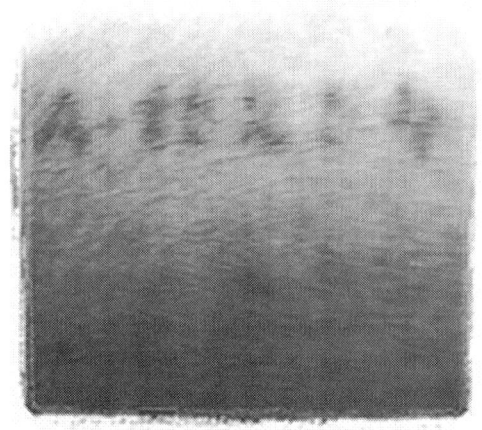

(Photo of Rachel's Left Arm with Tattoo #15254 – 2012)

(RTU - Welcoming speech (paraphrased) given by Obersturmführer Franz Hossler to a group of Greek Jews in the undressing room shortly before the group was led into the gas chamber to be killed:

"On behalf of the camp administration, I bid you welcome. This is not a holiday resort, but a labor camp.

Just as our soldiers risk their lives at the front to gain victory for the Third Reich, you will have to work here for the welfare of a new Europe.

How you tackle this task is entirely up to you.
The chance is there for every one of you. We shall
look after your health, and we shall also offer you
well-paid work.

After the war, we shall assess everyone according
to his merits and treat him accordingly.

Now, would you please all get undressed. Hang
your clothes on the hooks we have provided and
please remember your number [of the hook].

When you've had your bath, there will be a bowl
of soup and coffee or tea for all.

Oh yes, before I forget, after your bath, please
have ready your certificates, diplomas, school reports and any other documents so that we can
employ everybody according to his or her train-
ing and ability.")2

(Arrival Platform at Auschwitz - Carl's Brother Nathan Worked Here)

(Greek Jews Arriving in Auschwitz)

Rachel continues:

We stayed in long barracks without windows. We slept on floors. The barracks were empty and dark. There was no light or windows.

There was a big box in the middle of the room that was the toilet. The smell was always bad. There was no privacy.

We sewed uniforms for the Germans. Everyone had a part to do. I sewed the pockets.

At night we stood in line for a cup of soup. There was a big barrel of soup. We got a little bit of soup. Then, we would go to the barracks and sleep.

RTU:

How is it, do you think, you avoided....

Rachel:

I didn't avoid it. Nobody could avoid it. I was in the right place at the right time to survive. You could not hide.

Every morning they would have inspections. We were counted as we raised our hands.

Sometimes big ranking officers came in with those beautiful terrible uniforms and shiny boots. We were so afraid of them.

These officers would select,"You go to the left. You go to the right." You never knew the next thing.

I saw Adolph Eichman and Dr. Josef Mengele and many other high-ranking SS officers. They would come to make their special selections.

What Was Behind the Fierce Gaze of Dr. Josef Mengele?

(Dr. Josef Mengele circa 1940)

Rachel:

Carl, my future husband, stood before Dr. Mengele. Twice, Mengele stopped and looked into Carl's eyes. But, Carl was not taken.

(RTU - The notorious Nazi, Dr. Josef Mengele, was a physician who studied, among many things, human anthropology. He was known as the "Angel of Death."

Mengele survived the war to be secreted away to Argentina. His remains were positively identified in the 1980s. Dr. Mengele had been high on the most-wanted list of former Nazi Party officials.

Rachel's future husband, Carl Rosen-
berg, vividly remembered standing naked in a line of a hundred men.

Carl waited five hours on that chilly, wet September day. It was the eve of Rosh Hoshanah, the Jewish New Year.

Precisely at 9 a.m., Dr. Mengele and about 20 other Nazi S.S. officers arrived.

Mengele said to the 800 assembled men in 8 rows of 100, "You Jews, I'm here this morning to tell you what will be done to you.

Tomorrow is your New Year, and I have to tell you the ancient Jews sacrificed cattle for an offering to G-d.

Nowadays, in the Third Reich, we do not offer cattle. We offer you instead. Some of you will be selected by me as an offering for the new year."

Mengele proceeded to exam each of the 800 men, staring into their eyes. Carl remembered vividly Mengele's fierce and deep gaze into his eyes.

Mengele stood and paused over Carl twice, looking deeply into his eyes each time before moving on.)[3]

(RTU - At that time, Carl did not know that Mengele had an interest in heterochromia, a condition in which eyes have different colors.

Alexander the Great had heterochromia.

Mengele's gaze was for a reason. Mengele was looking for subjects to study. Mengele also studied twins.)[4]

RTU (returning to Rachel):

Did they tell you what they were doing?

Rachel:

I remember women talking about Mengele's experiments. He would take women to a special barracks and perform experiments on their female organs.

Many of the women could not bear children after the war. I met some of these women after the war.

We didn't know nothing. They didn't tell us anything. We didn't talk to anyone. We never had a pencil, a paper, a book to read.

We didn't even know what day it was.

We never heard reports of how the fighting was going. We did come to believe that the Americans were coming. But, it was only a rumor.

I kept busy by working. I did a little sewing. We didn't talk to the soldiers. We only saw the SS ladies. The women guards went out of their way to be mean to us.

Nobody ever talked about what they were going to do to us or what was to be.

What Did You See?

(Extermination oven at Auschwitz)

RTU:

What did you see? Did you see anything in the camp?

Rachel:

I walked by when they were not burning people. I walked by and saw the exactly empty gas chambers in Auschwitz.

RTU:

Tell me what you saw?

Rachel:

I saw a very big, very big brick gas chamber. It showed where the gas came out. There was a small door where people went in.

Whoever got in fell and got burned. Whenever they got 100 or 200 people, they took them to the gas chamber and then burned them.

There were black flames coming out of the oven smokestacks day and night, because they brought hundreds from Europe.

We knew what it was at the time. Then there were all these ashes. Even after the war, you could see the ashes. My sister, Bluma, saw them on a return visit after the war.

My mom was killed right away in a gas chamber (Treblinka) in such a way. She was with my youngest brother, Motel, who went with her into the gas chamber.

It was Yom Kippur when she died with her little boy.

They referred to us by our numbers. Every morning they counted heads at 6:00 a.m.

(Female SS Guards at Auschwitz)

(RTU - Rachel said this is exactly how they looked.The uniform would most likely be gray. The women SS used the same colored uniforms as the regular German Army.

This has contributed to the thought that the SS units were part of the regular German army. They were not.

The women SS were much more fanatical and devoted to Hitler than soldiers in the regular army.

The SS could be counted on to carry out the most heinous and cruel assignments as ordered. The SS fighting units were known for their fierce fighting, hand-to-hand combat and fighting to the death if necessary.)

Rachel continues:

The female SS guards were the same as they had been in the other camps. They were mean.

In Auschwitz, we knew we were there to be killed. Today it is you. Tomorrow it's me. There was no religion. No ceremonies, not even in secret.

We did not know what day it was. There was no Shabbat (Sabbath). No G-d.

There was a time when we carried seventy-five pound blocks in and out because the Germans were building.

Then, they would take us back to the barracks. Sometimes, before dark, we would lie on the sand around the barracks.

We would look at the sky and wondered who would survive. Would we ever be free? We saw people in the distance.

There were electric barbed wire fences. But, we could see through them. When we saw the birds, we wanted to be like them.

People would go out and touch the electric fence in order to kill themselves. It happened all the time.

There were about 1,400 women in my barracks. In the middle of the barracks was a box. If someone had to use the toilet, they went to that box.

People had to endure the smell. There was no privacy. We never saw water to clean or wash.

None of us had our periods (menses). Maybe it was because we were too skinny or perhaps the Germans put something in the food.

We would dream about romance. Now we were seventeen and eighteen and had never known about boys.

We stayed in long barracks without windows. We slept on floors. The barracks were empty and dark. There was no light.

The Holocaust Scream

Rachel:

At this time, my younger brother, Jacob, joined up with me. He slept with me in the barracks. I was three years in Auschwitz with my little brother.

A few women were able to keep children with them in the barracks. Not many made the connection with their children. It was dangerous and often sad when we did.

Jacob took care of the Germans' gooses (geese). Many times, he was able to bring me a small amount of food.

Auschwitz had a big hangar full of clothes. They took the clothes from the ones that were gassed.

One day, I went into the hangar and cut off some sleeves to use to cover Jacob's legs. It was cold.

A week later, Dr. Mengele inspected us in a line. Jacob was standing next to me.

There were cars like Hummers in the distance to take the ones they chose to the gas chamber.

They chose every other person that day. They pulled Jacob into the selection line and he started to scream. I screamed too.

I begged them to take me too. We both knew what was happening. I was Jacob's protector.

My little Jacob and I reached out and grabbed hands. I held his hand as tight as I could.

I begged for the Germans to take me. They kicked and kicked me until I had to let go of Jacob's hand. He was led away screaming my name.

After a few hours, the cars with the selections were taken to the gas chamber. I remember hearing Jacob crying for me even when he was out of sight.

They didn't take me, because I was good enough to work.

Sixty years later, I can still hear his cry, his scream, my little Jacob calling for me.

Losing Jacob was the biggest hurt I had in the six years while I was in the camps. I loved him more than life. He was healthy, happy and gorgeous.

Later, a close friend's 12-year-old son dedicated his Bar Mitzvah (Rite of Passage Ritual) to Jacob, because Jacob did not have a Bar Mitzvah. His name was Jacob too.

(RTU - If ever there was a place where Death and Love fought each other, it was on this terrible assembly ground in Oswiezim, Poland. There was no ambiguity, no uncertainty, those primal forces rising against each other.

I have heard Rachel discuss this battle with death. Each time, I am unable to utter a single word. I am aware of the silence, but nothing comes. Words may never come.

How about you? How did The Scream affect you? I would like to know how you feel as would Rachel. You could leave a comment at:

www.theholocaustscream.com

The road is long.....

Jacob Vann's Loving Tribute to Rachel's Lost Brother, Jacob Boiman

HE AIN'T HEAVY

HE'S MY BROTHER

(If I am burdened at all, I am burdened with sadness .....So on we go)(25)

(Text of address by Jacob Vann, son of Dr. and Mrs. John Vann of Omaha, NE. Presented by Jakob Vann at his Bar Mitzvah on his 13th birthday in 2010.)

In Loving Memory of Jacob Boiman

I'm glad you're all here. I am having my Bar Mitzvah in loving memory of Jacob Boiman, the younger brother of Mania Freidman, my friend Rachel Rosenberg and Bluma Polanski.

When the Boimans were separated, Mania and Bluma were taken together.

Their mother and youngest brother, Motel, had left them a few weeks earlier, to go to a nearby village where their mother felt safe.

Rachel and Jacob were deported from Szalkev Concentration Camp, which is where they were for a few weeks after being taken, also where they had relative comfort, to Blizyn Concentration Camp.

Blizyn was a nightmare. They were cold, hungry and dirty.

While Rachel had to carry cement blocks for construction, Jacob tended to the animals. Jacob would feed and clean the geese, ducks, chickens and pigs.

Sometimes, when he was feeling brave, Jacob would bring Rachel back an egg from one of the poultry.

Then, Rachel and Jacob were moved to Auschwitz Concentration Camp, where Jacob met his end. Rachel, who had been his protector, took his death very hard.

One day, they were standing around, when the SS, who targeted the young, came over and took him (Jacob) away.

Rachel cried and begged for him to be let go, but the SS just grabbed her and threw her down.

The only thing they would let her do was put a sweater over his shoulders so that he wouldn't be cold.

Jacob was twelve and a half years old when he was taken and murdered. I am having my Bar Mitzvah in honor of this young Holocaust victim, who never had the chance to have a Bar Mitzvah.

Rachel continues:

Can you believe that?

How Does a Piece of Bread and Risk-Taking Lead to Bluma and Mania?

Rachel:

The Germans had children in their own homes. How could they be that way to us?

Carl's other brother, Nathan, worked on the platform where the new people arrived in Auschwitz.

There was a barracks for the clothing and even a separate barracks for human hair. I even heard they took the gold fillings from the teeth of those they had killed.

One day, Nathan tossed me a piece of bread. He threw it to me over the electric wires. I cut the piece of bread and placed it in my bosom.

A few days later, I saw two women. I saw that they were my sisters, Bluma and Mania. I screamed at them. I hadn't seen them before in the camp.

I waited until the guards were looking the other way. I ran into the forbidden part near the barbed wire and threw the bread to them.

The bread was so hard that Mania cut one of her fingers trying to slice the bread. The bread was old and hard as steel. Her finger lost some function.

She had a stiff finger which stayed with her for the rest of her life.

One day in Auschwitz, while we were in line, the supervisor called my number. Mine was the only number called.

I thought, "This is it. They are going to kill me." I wondered what kind of death they were going to give me. I was so scared.

Sometimes when we were working outside the camps, the Germans would lead some of our group away into the forest and kill them for no reason.

Instead, the supervisor reported that I was a good worker. I was given a black uniform, which meant I was a good worker.

I remember being afraid. I remember knowing there was no tomorrow for us. I don't remember if I had any dreams while I was in the camp.

Now, I have dreams about the camp that upset and disturb me. Sometimes, I have trouble falling asleep. To this day police officers, sirens and large dogs make me afraid.

During my time in the camps, none of us ever cried or screamed. We never had any fights.

We never hurt or hit anybody. We were like little sheep, like animals for the slaughter.

We never talked to any of the officers or the SS ladies. They never talked to us in a friendly conversation.

They were very mean and brutal to us. When they had to tell us something, they spoke Polish.

Between us, we spoke Yiddish and to the Germans we would have spoken German, although I don't remember ever speaking to the Germans.

How Did Rachel Manage to Hide in Auschwitz?

Rachel:

I kept this view throughout my times in the camps. This fear of being touched by men in some way may have helped me.

I never spoke to the male guards in the camps at any time. I would intentionally hang around the back and edges of groups to make myself less noticeable.

RTU:

Rachel, do you remember any of the high-ranking SS women officers? Did you ever see a women with a bloodhound, not a German shepherd dog?

Dr. Mengele had a woman physician who also made selections. Her name was Margot Drechler. She would have been in the front with her bloodhound.

Rachel:

I can only remember one time that I saw a woman in front with a big dog. I don't remember her name.

(RTU - Unrepentant Dr. Margot Drechler was hanged a few days after the end of the war.)

Rachel continues:

I always tried to stay away from any gatherings, commotions or the front lines.

I began to notice that sometimes the Germans would come and take people out to be killed. Who they chose at that time made no sense.

I noticed that if you were near the front of the lines, you were more likely to be chosen. I would try to be at the back of the crowd.

Whenever I could, I would drop back into my camp barracks at the last minute. I was out of sight.

No one saw me do this. Everyone was watching what was going on in the front. I didn't see a lot of what took place.

I would hide in the barracks until all the others came back. No one told me to do this. No one joined me in the hiding. I told no one, not even those close to me in the camp.

Did Carl Really Save Bluma at the Last Minute?

Rachel:

On one of these selections occasions, I had managed to stay back in the barracks. The Germans came and selected 15 people to be exterminated.

My sister Bluma was one of them.

Sometimes, Dr. Mengele came and made selections. Mengele chose my sister Bluma. Maybe it was because she was skinny?

Perhaps the Germans thought skinny workers were not strong and not good workers?

She was placed in a building to be taken away the next morning. It was cold and there was deep snow. All the time Bluma was cold and barefooted.

(RTU - Carl Rosenberg, Rachel's future husband, worked as a tailor for the SS. He was only able to rescue Bluma this time. The SS officer gave Bluma to Carl after Carl asked for her.

He asked the officer to let her live a little longer, because she was his cousin. This took place about

15 minutes before Bluma was to leave with the other condemned in the group of 15. This time, the Germans wanted exactly 15 prisoners to be taken away to be killed.

Carl was a master tailor and had been put to work making custom officer's uniforms for the SS. It was for that reason that the Germans knew him and allowed Bluma to leave the building where she was being held.

Carl also threatened the lower- ranking SS officers with trouble from their superiors if Bluma was not set free.

Carl did excellent tailoring for the top SS Officers in the camp. The officers came to like Carl, in a way, because of his work. Carl could talk with the top officers.

This time, Carl took a big chance and was able to rescue Bluma. It was a bluff, but it worked with the low-ranking guards at sunrise that morning.

Carl wrote about this and his camp experiences in his book: As God Is My Witness (Carl Rosenberg 1990).

The guards, who came to escort the doomed, noticed that one was missing from the count.

Finally, they just let it go. The guards took the remaining 14 off to be killed.)

Rachel continues:

This selection process was a very frequent happening. Anyone could be chosen for no reason whatsoever.

All of us had a terrible feeling and did not know what was going to happen next.

Where to Next? Auschwitz to.....

(German Railcar circa 1940)

Rachel:

In 1945, I left Auschwitz for Czechoslovakia. We travelled by train with about 150 people packed into each railcar.

We could only stand body-to-body. I remember it was cold.

(RTU - According to reports, the German rail system billed the Nazis and were paid in terms of passenger mile units.

The more people crammed into one car, the more money the railroad made. The German railroad system kept meticulous records.

Many of these bills for passenger mile units have survived the war. The existence of these papers is, in a way, a testament.

These documents are evidence of what the Nazis had done. The people were packed like sardines, the rail bills are proof of this.

Rachel continues:

On the boxcar, they allowed the door to be opened once a day. Some of the older people didn't make it. They just threw their bodies out.

My aunt Hanna was with me in one of the rail-cars. She had a piece of bread. The other prisoners mobbed Hanna and killed her for the bread.

We were in the same car and I saw her being killed. I named my daughter Annie after her.

(RTU - Annie is the English equivalent of Hannah.)

Rachel continues:

On the way, all we had to eat was a spoonful of sugar each day. We must have had water, but I don't remember the details.

I do remember the Germans would open the train doors once a day. When they did, almost always I could see American planes overhead in V-shaped (flying) formations.

We could hear the bombs. We wished the planes would bomb near our location to help us.

We were for anything, even bombs,that would finish our situation. We hoped partisans would come to the train at night, but it never happened.

After 13 days on the train, we came to a camp in Czechoslovakia. The Germans had set up small camps along the way and would assign 150 here, 150 there.

The name of this, my last camp, was Naderland (sp?). My sisters were not with me.

I had beautiful long hair. When they opened the door of the train car, one of the SS women grabbed my hand and put me in a room in a building all by myself.

I had no idea why.

At night, the door opened. She had a pair of sheep scissors. She took off all my hair. I couldn't ask why.

She gave me a black bandalino (colored rag) to wear around my head.

One day, a German soldier came up to me and gave me a package. My cousin, Rachel Karpman, was in another camp and knew where I was. The soldier told me the package was from Rachel Karpman.

There was no note. I don't know how Rachel was able to get the soldier to do that.

In the package was a piece of bread. It was all secretive for her to give me that bread. Rachel was a saint.

She was wonderful. She was smart. She loved me. We were first cousins.

"Rachel, may you rest in peace." She was my very best friend in Omaha. We loved each other very much. I miss her.

When I have a chance, I visit her grave and cry my heart out.

We were there (Czechoslovakia) a couple of months. Every morning they would check our work. One day a SS lady told us that it would not be long until we were liberated.

She said it was a secret.

We did not believe the rumors that the war might be coming to an end.

We never sensed or got excited about the war ending for us until one morning we woke up and the German guards were gone and the Russians were walking around in the camp.

There had been no bombings or shootings. Suddenly, the Russians were there. We had no sense of tomorrow while we were under the Germans. There was no tomorrow. Hope was cruel.

What is Freedom? No More Physical Cage but.......

Rachel:

While in Czechoslovakia, we were assigned by the Germans to work in an ammunition factory. We were very hungry.

After working in the ammunition factory for a few weeks, the Germans also put us to work in a large potato cellar sorting large and small potatoes.

This was additional work to what I was doing in the ammunition factory.

There was a German guard at the door of the potato cellar. One day, I stole a potato and put it in my bosom. For over a week, I ate that potato a little bit at a time, a bite a day.

On May 5th 1945, the Russians came and told us we were liberated. Our camp was not liberated by the Americans.

It was liberated by the Russians. I looked and saw Russian soldiers in our camp. They were good to us.

They told us we were free. What does that mean? I had no hair.

(RTU – Auschwitz Concentration Camp had been liberated on January 27, 1945, by the Russians. January 27 has become International Holocaust Remembrance Day.)

The Simple Things in Life

Rachel:

Later, after we had been freed, about 10 of us went into that potato cellar and brought up potatoes. We gathered together and found a large kettle.

We made a big fire for the 10 of us. We all were 18 to 20 years old. This was our first meal since we were taken.

The Russians didn't say anything.

This was my first real meal in 6 years. Sometimes even today, I enjoy a raw potato.

So.... Why Does the Struggle Continue?

Rachel:

In the meantime, we were in Czechoslovakia. I thought I would find my sisters, Bluma and Mania. I looked for Mania. I looked for Bluma.

There was no Bluma. No Mania. I didn't find them at first. Later, I did when they were brought to my location.

The authorities took us to orphanage buildings in Prague, the capital of Czechoslovakia. Again, I was separated from my sisters when we were sorted in the middle of the road.

While we were in those orphanage houses in Czechoslovakia, there were 6-7 of us in a group of cousins (girls only).

We decided to take a trip to Poland to see what was going on, to go upstairs and see what was left of our belongings.

I don't remember our clothes. We probably had shoes. We probably took potatoes to eat along the way.

We started to walk through the woods at night. We didn't have any pillows or blankets. We bundled up together to keep warm.

Nobody saw us. Nobody stopped us. It was a long walk to central Poland. It took 3 days of hard and fast walking. We were not afraid.

(RTU - There were subsequent reports of Jews being killed as they returned from the concentration camps. There were many reasons for this.

Under the circumstances, the girls were not as safe as they might have thought. It is 100+ miles from the Czech border to Wolanow.)

Rachel continues:

We knocked at the door of my old home. After the war started, the Poles took over all the houses. The lady asked who we were.

We told her. I remember the storage in the basement. She let us go up into the attic. We found family pictures and took them with us.

The lady probably fed us. I remember that she told us, "Listen kids, if you want to live, go back where you came from."

The reason was that the Poles were afraid we would take back our homes.

We did not visit any other houses. We left at night. We lost all the pictures. It was raining heavily and the pictures and albums were too heavy.

We were resigned to the fact that we could not do anything about the loss of all our possessions. We left as fast as we could.

It was a long hard walk back to Czechoslovakia and the orphanages.

It was about this time that my sisters joined with me in Prague. Carl, my future husband, did as well.

I don't know how he found me. He told me he had been looking all over for me and would not stop until he found me.

What About Living Among the Germans? Stuttgart and Landsberg am Lech

Rachel:

The Americans eventually shipped us out to Stuttgart, Germany. The city had been heavily bombed.

Rachel:

We lived in barracks until we got our visas to America. We had heard that the U.S. was the best place in the world. Money grew on trees. We didn't want to go anywhere else.

RTU:

Did you know about Israel and what was going on there?

Rachel:

Yes, I did. I didn't want to go to Israel. I was tired of the struggle and constant problems.

Carl wanted to go to Israel and join the Irgun (unofficial Israeli guerilla counter-terrorism unit noted for its revenge tactics.

The Irgun believed that every Jew had the right to enter Palestine and only active retaliation against the Arabs would preserve the Jewish State.

The paramilitary Irgun was absorbed into the Israeli Defense Forces in 1948.)

Rachel continues:

Carl wanted to fight. I told him I would not go to Israel.

Next, we went to Landsberg Am Lech (Germany). My Carl, with 2 other men, opened a tailor shop there. We lived in barracks that had housed German soldiers.

In Landsberg Am Lech, we didn't go out. Our little group of cousins and friends didn't have any fun. I worked eight hours in a shirt factory.

We had no friends, even among the Jews. No one knocked on our door. People were not nice to us.

No one asked how we were doing. No one asked any questions about what had happened to us.

The Americans weren't nice to us. They were not mean. They just left us isolated. We felt alone and abandoned.

About two thousand of us sewed shirts from scratch for the Americans. We were not paid. We did not see a dollar.

We were given Care Packages (boxes of essentials from the U.S.). I knew I was good at sewing. They had a big picture of me, like a poster. It showed me working in a factory.

We all had separate rooms. Little by little, we branched out. Mania and I got married.

Marriage to Carl Rosenberg

Rachel:

Carl and I got married in Landsberg am Lech, Germany, on July 20th, 1946. You know how it is. I was 20. He was very much in love with me.

I didn't really care that much for him. He took very good care of me, my two sisters and several cousins.

I found a piece of white material and made my wedding dress. I don't know who made the wedding arrangements.

There was a Rabbi and a small reception. We didn't have any money. Later, my sisters and cousins would use the same dress for their wed-dings.

On April 18th of 1948, I had my first child, Mor-ris. It wasn't like it is here in the states. I was in a room with about 10 other women giving birth.

Mania moved to Israel. A few years later, I paid her family's way to come back to Omaha. It took two to three years to get a visa to come to Ameri-ca.

How I Discovered Love - My Husband Carl

Rachel:

Carl is my relative. When he was a young man, he lived in Wolanow with his family. Later, he came and took them all to Warsaw.

He lived in Warsaw a couple years. He was an officer in the Polish Army.

When the war broke out, instead of going to Russia with his family, he came to the little town where he was born.

He came to Wolanow. He had a mother, a father, two sisters and two brothers.

Carl was a master tailor. He learned tailoring in Warsaw when he was fifteen or sixteen years old. He had an uncle in Warsaw, who taught him tailoring.

When Carl first came to Wolanow, I was about ten years old. Carl was ten years older than me. I was ten years old and he was twenty years old.

We were together in my home in Wolanow. He took me around. I had just started to develop.

He felt my little breast and since then, he just fell madly in love with me, just madly.

Later, Carl would tell people about the time he touched me and fell in love with me.

During my time in the concentration camps, I never saw Carl. He was in Auschwitz at the same time, but I never saw him.

After the war, when they brought us into the orphanage houses, Carl showed up. He had looked me up. He wanted to be with me.

I didn't care strongly for him. He was ten years older than me. He wasn't the guy I would have liked to be with.

My two sisters, Mania and Bluma, were very much against me marrying Carl.

But then, I had a cousin, which I adored. She was very, very smart. Her name was Rachel Karpman.

She said to me, "Listen Rachel, you are a beautiful young lady. You might get hurt by someone really bad. So in order to protect you, I want you to marry Carl."

Her words touched me. I didn't care strongly for Carl. I just loved her. I adored her. Because of her and my respect for her, I decided to take her advice.

She was very smart and understood things I didn't. She was kinda my protector. Everyone wanted to take a bite of me, because I was beautiful.

People would often touch a part of me, my hair, my eyes. I didn't know why. I was shy and naïve.

Then, I listened to Rachel Karpman. I didn't want to break her words.

I said to myself, "Well, if Rachel told me to marry Carl, even if I wasn't in love with him, it would be okay for me."

But then, because of Rachel Karpman, I married Carl.

I don't regret marrying Carl at all.

- He was handsome.

- He treated me softly.

- He was a good father.

- He was a good provider, a great master tailor.

- He was tall.

- He loved me with a love like nothing else in the world.

My mother had told me to never marry a tailor. In Poland before the war, tailors were looked down on as a profession. Tailors in Poland were always poor and barely getting by.

As it turned out, tailors were highly regarded in the United States. Tailoring was an honored profession. We could make good money. We were professionals.

I lived with my Carl as husband and wife for sixty-two years. We had three beautiful children. It was a good marriage. I lost him five years ago and I still miss him very much.

RTU:

And so it sounds like you discovered love somewhere along the line?

Rachel:

Yes, and later on I got used to him and I loved him very very much to the end of his life.

It's true.

Coming to America

Rachel:

We left for the United States. The ship's name was the General Houser (sp?). I was seasick the whole time because of the ship's movements.

Bluma was looking for a husband, but didn't find one.

We came through Ellis Island. I noticed lights, people in cars, people well-dressed. We couldn't speak English.

They had someone speak Jewish (Yiddish) to us. They asked if we had someone to claim us or sponsor us. We didn't have a sponsor at the time we first arrived in New York.

Before we left Germany, they gave each of us $100. I bought a set of Rosenthal china. I recently gave the set to my daughter, Annie.

All of us bought umbrellas. We were told we could not buy umbrellas on the way.

No one gave us any good advice as to what to bring with us. We just came. Now I can laugh about it.

We came to the United States with no money. No one had any money to speak of when we landed in the United States.

The Jewish Community Center in Omaha sponsored us after we came to the United States.

We travelled by train to Omaha (Nebraska). We were greeted by Sadie Newman. May she rest in peace. She had her hair down. She had a fur coat and drove a car.

Being cooped up in a death camp for six years, I had never seen a lady drive a car. We drove into Omaha. The lights were on.

I saw houses with big windows, cars, dresses, pocket books, which I did not have.

I told Sadie that someday I wanted a house with big windows, a fur coat, my hair done, and a pocket book.

The start in Omaha was very hard. We didn't speak English. They put us in an apartment on 24th street. All of us, including Bluma, were in one room.

There used to be a potato market on 16th street. They (the Jewish Federation) took us there and gave us a little money.

There was a man named Friedman, who had a furniture store. He brought me a little oven so I could cook for my child.

The Jewish Community Center gave us linens and pillows. We just stayed in our rooms.

Mr. Paul Veret was very good to us. He was Executive Director of the Jewish Community Center. Paul Veret put us into the Clarinda apartment building.

After 6 months, Mr. Veret told us it was time to find a job.

I had my Morris (first child - baby boy born 1948). I put him in day care, but he cried too much. I had to keep him with me.

Carl was looking for a job. Sistak was the biggest tailor in Omaha. He did not want to hire Carl, because he couldn't speak English.

We went to Mr. Veret. He said he was going to get Carl a job. Mr. Veret found a dry cleaning establishment. Carl went to work for them. Every morning, Carl was picked up.

Carl put in zippers, made alterations, shortened pants and let out waists. After a couple of weeks, the owner said to Carl that he was so talented, he should find a place of his own.

About this time, I went to work sewing at Pendleton's. It was a terrible day and experience. I was so afraid that I was not working hard enough to please the supervisor.

I could not relax. I came home exhausted and told Carl this was not the life I wanted. We decided to open our own store. We wanted Mr. Veret to find us a store.

Before we came to the US, we bought four Pfaff sewing machines (trade name of top-line German sewing machines). I don't know whose idea it was.

(RTU – Each of these sewing machine could perform a separate function. They still work.)

Rachel continues:

The machines were brand new. When we told Mr. Veret, he said he was going to rent us a store.

At first, we had no income. We were thrown out of house after house because we couldn't pay rent. In one house, the lady came into the room in the middle of the night.

We were all asleep. She said, "You get out." She was drunk. She ordered us out of the house. I asked her where we could go? We left in the morning.

We told Mr. Veret about this. He helped us rent a store on Leavenworth Street. We put our sewing machines there.

Mr. Veret said the Federation did not have a lot of money for us. We took all our belongings and moved into the basement with our shop above us.

The rent was $90. There was no kitchen, no beds, no stove or tables, just a room with a toilet. We were all settled. We stayed 6 months in that basement.

The Federation did pay three months of our rent. We did very well. Bluma babysat with Morris, while Carl and I worked in the shop.

My break in Omaha came when Vergie Meyers, who owned the Countryside Village (small strip mall), went to Boy's Town and told them about Carl.

Boy's Town sent us a lot of business.

It was at this time, we began to do a lot of alterations for Boys Town. We worked maybe 4 weeks from 6 in the morning until 10 at night on work from Boys Town.

We Have Money

Rachel:

We did their (Boys Town's) shortenings, alterations, zippers and let-outs.

One day they came in with a piece of paper, which they said was for me. I didn't know what it meant. I had no money in the bank.

I called Sadie. She started to cry. Sadie said, "Rachel, we have money." It was a check for $250.

I don't know how that worked. Somehow they knew to send me the money. We had no stationery or billing procedures.

Sadie was a real estate agent. She took the money and bought us a house across the street on Leavenworth. It was a one story house with a basement. It still stands.

Mr. Veret from the Jewish Community Center paid the first month's mortage. The payment was $90.

I rented out the top floor for $90, which made my monthly mortgage payment. The rest of us lived downstairs. I was with Carl, Morris my baby and my sister Bluma.

After maybe three months, the upstairs couple moved. I went out and bought a baby bed for Morris.

I noticed that there were times that I would find Carl upstairs in tears. Once he told me, "Thank G-d that my baby is free and has a bed to sleep and we are not afraid of anything."

(Rachel and Morris circa 1950)

We had our bedroom. Bluma stayed with us. I began to work with Carl. Bluma went to work in a mattress factory. She made a few dollars.

Bluma met Joe Polanski. They had a wedding in the Jewish Community Center. The Center helped with the arrangements.

Bluma wore a borrowed wedding dress and so did I. We didn't have any fancy clothes at that time. After the wedding, Bluma moved out.

Business was good. We stayed on Leavenworth Street. I worked with Carl day and night. The four Pfaff sewing machines helped us a lot.

The Jewish Federation got me a lady who stayed in the store. She spoke with the customers because we couldn't understand English.

The lady was with us a few weeks, until we got to know the language.

That's when we started to make a few dollars.

RTU:

Who ran the cash register? Who took the money if you didn't speak English?

Rachel:

The lady did. The lady took care of the cash register and the customers. Then, we started to learn English.

We didn't have time to go to school. We did it ourselves.

I don't remember where we got the money to buy groceries.

We didn't have a cash register. The lady, in our store, gave us some money, maybe from alterations. I don't remember.

When we moved into our first home, we didn't have any furniture. We went out and bought some old furniture.

The survivors with no place to stay,slept with us.

There could be as many as ten people staying with us at one time. We had cots. We also had one of the first air conditioners for everyone to use.

We didn't charge anyone a thing for staying with us.

We would use the buses. We bought kosher food. We also bought half-priced bread. The clothes weren't important. We made our own.

A few years later, we bought a duplex. I rented out the other side, which made my payments. We bought a used car, a yellow Chevrolet.

It was about this time that Carl and I had our other two children. Annie Rose is my daughter and our middle child.

Today she lives in Minneapolis with her family. We are very close and she helps me a lot especially now as I grow older.

Annie and her husband Kenny have a successful business in Minneapolis. I always like to know that my children are successful and getting along.

My youngest child is named Stuart. He is a successful stock broker in Los Angeles.

Although he is farther away, Stuart checks on me all the time or I scold him. Stuart helps manage my money.

I lost my oldest child, Morris, about five years ago. I miss him very much. I love Annie and Stuart very much. I am glad they are in my life and close to me.

Why Was Being in Omaha Hard at First? Socially.......

Rachel:

There was an occasion that took place when we were new to Omaha. We knew it was Yom Kippur (Jewish Day of Atonement). It was holy to me. I remembered my home.

My father made it a special day. He was religious.

We always had passers-by to stay with us. My mother and father had black outfits.

I remember being a child on Kol Nidre (which means the annulment of all vows). I remember the cantor's melody. They said it was a Holy Day, which it is.

I told Bluma that we should go to the synagogue for Kol Nidre. Carl stayed with the baby. The synagogue was not far away.

The Jewish Community Center had given us clothes. They gave me a burgundy coat. Bluma had a blue coat. They gave us shoes, not walking shoes, shoes with high heels.

It was hard to walk. We had never worn high heels. We were in our 20's. They didn't give us stockings. I had a black pair of stockings. Bluma had a burgundy pair of stockings.

So, we walked to the Temple. People were coming in with fur coats, minks, and cars. It was October. When we walked into the synagogue, we saw chandeliers.

The Rabbi was dressed (for Kol Nidre). The Bimah (a raised platform for the Torah) was beautiful. People were beautifully dressed.

We heard the organ and started crying. We were not well- dressed. We looked terrible. We looked like the homeless.

It hurts 'til today. Nobody asked who we were or what we were doing there. It was sad. We went home crying all the way. The walk back was hard in the high heels.

Later, when we would sit at the Beth El (synagogue) cafeteria tables, people would get up and leave. I had paid for our dinner, but the people would not have anything to do with us.

They did this a lot for a long time. That is the way it was. They didn't see us. They just didn't like us. We weren't very well-dressed.

The Rabbi was Carl's good friend. Carl was always very religious.

RTU:

How about friends? Did you have any friends?

Rachel:

We didn't have any friends. Nobody had anything to do with us. I am sorry to say that many in the Omaha Jewish community were not nice to us for many years.

RTU:

This whole time?

Rachel:

All the time. They ignored us. They were ashamed of us. We were never invited to anyone's home to see how they lived.

One day Bluma said, "Let's go shopping." We went shopping. There was a Jewish lady who owned a lady's store.

Bluma tried on a white blouse that fit her perfectly. The blouse cost $2. It was size ten.

We didn't have the money. Bluma asked if she could have the blouse and that she would get a job and pay her back. The lady would not give her the blouse.

The lady said in Yiddish, "Girl, do you have any money?" The lady said, "No money. No blouse." Bluma and I always talk about this.

So, we were treated very poorly by many, when we came to the United States.

RTU:

Did anyone ever yell at you or call you names?

Rachel:

Nobody yelled at us. They would not have anything to do with us.

There Were Lighter Moments Too

Rachel:

One day, I went to a big giant grocery in Omaha. At that time, I couldn't speak English. I went in.

There was a sign, "Three-legged chicken." I didn't know what that means.

I went to the owner and I said, "Listen, I never heard before from a three-legged chicken."

He was laughing you won't believe. He explained to me that there were three pieces of chicken.

Then, he wanted to give me some lettuce. I told him I was not going to take the lettuce. Cows in Europe ate the lettuce.

He told me to try it, but I didn't. It was hard going.

Visiting a Holocaust Museum

Rachel:

I remember when I went to visit my sister Bluma in 1980. We went to see the Holocaust Museum in Miami.

When I walked in, I didn't think I would live through it. The hurt was tremendous.

The statues. There was a pond with water. In the middle of the pond was a hand with a number from Auschwitz. It was beautifully done in a way.

Then, I saw some statues made from peoples, moms holding babies. There was an aisle. There was music.

The whole time I was there, I was just crying, crying, crying. My sister and I were crying and holding each other.

One statue, which was very hard for me to see, was of a little boy. It reminded me, the way he was crying, of my brother Jacob.

I remember when they took him away. I could hear his screaming and I could see his face in those statues. I was devastated.

As we went farther, there were gas chambers. There were dead people made from steel. There were things of Auschwitz, the rail road.

That was a very hard picture for us to see. I hope, in my lifetime, I could go again and see Auschwitz in Poland.

In another place, there was another Holocaust museum. General Eisenhower wrote a wonderful poem, but I don't remember it.

(RTU - "The things I saw beggar description...The visual evidence and the verbal testimony of starvation, cruelty and bestiality were so overpowering...

I made the visit deliberately, in order to be in a position to give first hand evidence of these things if ever, in the future, there develops a tendency to charge these allegations to propaganda.")[5]

(Condensed from a paragraph in a letter that General Eisenhower wrote to General George C. Marshall on April 15, 1945.

This quote is part of a larger quote placed on a plaque outside the Holocaust Memorial Museum in Washington D.C.)

Rachel continues:

There were also statues of children when they were taken away to the gas chamber. Their mothers were holding them.

I do appreciate that they are building and showing the people what really has happened in World War 2, what Hitler did to the Jewish people.

The statues were made just like real people. You could see their faces, the mothers. You could see them crying. Under them were people begging for air before they put them to the gas chamber. It was a very emotional sight for me to see.

Until today, when I see a picture of Auschwitz, Theresienstadt or any of the four camps I was in, I burst with tears. It is very painful. It reminded me of my people; that little boy, my Jacob, on his knees, begging the SS to let him go.

They want to be with me. Those faces were made just like my little Jacob's face. Just like I remember and there were hundreds like them.

I don't know what kind of death they gave them. They had to take their clothes off. The German guards would say, "You take a shower."

And then, they got in. Then, they got gassed. They put the ashes out. The ashes are still at Auschwitz.

Should I Try the American Stock Market?

Rachel:

Well, we were in the store, we started making money. We learned English. I bought an investment house. Soon, I sold it and made some money.

I thought, buy property, not buy property. Somebody introduced me to buying stocks. I bought a little stock.

My first dollars I used to buy 100 shares of General Motors.

I kept buying and buying. I had three stock brokers giving me advice. But, I kinda watched the stocks. I still do today.

How I learned, I have no idea. I had a good eye, which one to buy.

One of my stock brokers advised me not to buy Union Pacific. I said, "I'm going to buy it and that's it." I have it 'til today. I get dividends from Union Pacific.

I did it all myself and I did good. That is why now I can afford to live in a very good assisted living place.

I decided what stocks to buy and sell. My husband Carl did not know what a stock is. I did it.

I bought and sold, bought and sold. I couldn't read. I didn't know English well.

I had what you might call intuition. I had a feeling and just knew. Name a good stock, El Paso (energy), General Motors, Google. I have it. I stayed with the big ones.

Once, I bought a stock called EMC. I put three thousand dollars into it. EMC grew and grew into $300,000 before 9-11.

I told my son Stuart to look into a property. My son bought a home in Southern California for $400K. Stuart didn't have a place to live at that time.

One of the owners of a nearby shopping mall had ignored me. I had helped her raise her kids. I decided not to invest with her and bought property in California.

Recently, that house was worth a lot of money.

What About Nazi Encounters in Omaha?

RTU:

Was there a time when you were living in Omaha or anywhere after you left the camps, when you felt threatened by anyone or anything?

Rachel:

Yes. A few years ago, I was speaking to a group in South Omaha. I don't remember the school.

The lady, after I finished the children (the six graders), came up to me and said, "Rachel, I have about 75-100 adults who want to hear your story."

They were all sitting and waiting for me to speak. I was not expecting it, but I made from the bad situation a good situation.

I said, "Be a good sport." I spoke to them for about an hour.

Then, a few weeks or two weeks later, I went out from my house and stepped on a little step. There was a big swastika with black markings.

I don't know what kind of paint they used. It was a big swastika on my sidewalk.

I got real scared and screamed. I called a friend and said, "Please help me." Then, we called the ADL (Anti-Defamation League).

The president of the ADL came in and comforted and held me. He told to not be afraid.

Then, we called the police. By that time, they couldn't find anyone. They searched. They did all kinds of things, but they don't know who it was.

And then, one time, about two or three years ago, we had a store, Carl's Tailors.

In the middle of the day, a couple, I don't know, three or four men, marched in with a flag. On the flag, was a big big swastika.

I started to scream. And I said, "What are you doing here? Get out of here." I grabbed the telephone and called the police.

By the time I called the police, they had gone. So I don't know if they found them or not.

A Knife at Rachel's Throat - The Mugging - Fast Thinking

RTU:

I heard that you have an experience, a mugging, in Omaha. Can you tell me about it?

Rachel:

It was 9:00 in the morning. There was a special sale on in one of the stores. I wasn't really dressed well. I put on a big shirt and pants.

At that time, I had a new Lexus (car). I drove by myself. I parked in the front of the shopping mall.

As I turned off the engine and had the keys in my hand, a man jumped into my car. He wore a gray outfit.

He said, "It's a holdup. Don't scream. Don't cry. Be quiet. I am desperate. I need money."

I was sitting there and didn't know what to do. He pushed me down on the seat. He said, "Give me your purse. I need money."

I had 80-90 dollars in my purse. He took the purse and took out all the money he could. He left the cards and the purse.

He said, "This is not enough." He took out a knife and put it straight to my throat.

He said, "I'm going to kill you. You give me your keys. Take me to your bank and get me big money."

When I heard this, I put the keys in my brassiere. He didn't see me move the keys.

I said, "I don't have the keys. I don't have a bank. I don't have big money. Why would you want to kill me?"

So, we began to struggle, like wrestling. He pushed me down, but it took a while. We were struggling, struggling, struggling. We were fighting.

I thought, "G-d help me. I am going to die in his hands."

He took out that knife and pointed to my throat. I was struggling to move away from the knife.

I am 4 feet 11 inches tall and weighed about 120 pounds. He was much bigger. But I wanted to live.

Finally, he had me down in the car. He stopped to light a cigarette. When I saw him light that cigarette, I opened the door and fell on the side-walk.

I did not scream at first and then I did. He ran away from the other side. The police never caught him.

I was interviewed on television about this. My advice is to always lock your doors.

The Second Generation of the Holocaust - 100% Affected

(Family Photo – Annie, Rachel, Stuart Morris and Carl circa 1960)

Rachel:

The second generation of the Holocaust, the children, no matter how brave or smart they are, they could be doctors, bankers, teachers, my daughter Annie is a teacher, they are all affected 100% by us, by the Holocaust.

RTU:

Rachel, I had occasion to talk to your daughter Annie. She said that when she was growing up, she didn't know about the Holocaust.

In fact, none of her cousins in the second generation knew about the Holocaust.

They all knew something was wrong. Something bad had happened. They didn't know the details for many, many years. What was going on?

Rachel:

Well, I was over-protective. I never...

RTU:

What do you mean over-protective?

Rachel:

I was afraid to tell them what I had been through. I never, when I was younger, I never, never, ever talked to my children about the Holocaust.

I never talked to anyone about the Holocaust. I kept it between me and my husband. Carl and I talked a lot about being in the camps.

When Annie went to Pepperdine University in Los Angeles, she was 18 years old. In a class, they discussed and taught her about the Holocaust.

They showed her a tattoo number. Annie remembered that her mom and father both had such numbers. She couldn't understand why.

Until today, she is mad at me. Why didn't I tell her who I was?   I was screaming at night. I had nightmares. Her life was different from her girl-friends.

She (Annie) was a good student. We worked very hard to dress her the best that could be.

RTU:

Apparently both you and Carl agreed not to men-tion the Holocaust to anyone, because the cousins didn't know either.

Rachel:

No. We didn't.

When my children were grown up, one day my Annie left to a girlfriend's. I went crazy. I cried. I was just hysterical.

In my mind, you know, my little brother was tak-en away from me in Auschwitz. He was a thriving, a beautiful young 12-year-old.

This kinda haunted me, that someone would take away my children.

This is why I never talked about my ordeal about being in the concentration camp. 'Til recently, I was always afraid somebody was going to take a child away from me.

I couldn't even have a pet. I am afraid if I don't see the pet all the time, I get panicky and scared that something has happened to it.

RTU:

How did you correct your children when they were young and they made mistakes? Say they wanted something. Would you give it to them, most likely?

Rachel:

Yes, I gave them everything.

RTU:

They wanted?

Rachel:

They wanted. Because I never got anything from my parents. So, I thought we worked very hard to give them everything they needed.

They had education. They had cars. They had everything.

RTU:

Looking back, do think that was a good idea?

Rachel:

No, it wasn't. But I didn't know any better.

RTU:

Why wasn't it a good idea?

Rachel:

Well, because here in the United States, you make them grow up. You make them be independent.

I didn't know that. I always wanted to keep my children close to me. But it didn't work.

In my old age, right now, I can't understand how I am all by myself. I am here alone. I don't understand this.

RTU:

Don't you think, though, that is kinda the way of the world in the United States?

Rachel:

Yes, this is the way of the world, but I didn't visualize this. I thought I would always gonna be with my kids.

RTU:

They would be living like in a little town in Poland.

Rachel (laughing):

Yes.

RTU:

Everyone would live together.

Rachel (laughing):

Yes. That's true.

RTU:

No one would ever leave.

Rachel (laughing):

Yes, that's right.

RTU (laughing):

But this is the United States.

Rachel (laughing):

This is the United States. But I didn't understand. Yeah. That's true. That's true. Yeah.

What About Rachel's Encounter with Steven Spielberg and "Schindler's List"?

RTU:

I heard you and Carl both met with Steven Spielberg before he made the movie, "Schindler's List". Tell me about your experience.

Rachel:

When I was in Los Angeles, I happened to meet Steven Spielberg. His mother had a restaurant called the *Milky Way*. The restaurant was strictly kosher.

He took me to his mother's restaurant. One side was a milky side, the other side was for meat. I said, "My G-d, in the United States!"

I know that when I was growing up in a home that was kosher, we had special dishes for milk and for meat.

(RTU- There is a Torah-based prohibition against mixing milk and meat products.)

So, we went to his mother's restaurant. He paid for our meal. He was very nice to us. He was a nice pleasant man.

I said to him, "Steven, you are a director. You are a big shot and you want to talk to me, a survivor from Auschwitz?"

And he took me around. He gave me a little hug.

We spent about half a day with him. We told all kinds of stories about what we went through when I was in the concentration camps.

And of course, he made that movie "Schindler's List", which I have never seen. Maybe someday I can see it with some of my friends.

It will be hard for me to look at, because I have been through all that. I am not sure I want to see it for the memories.

I have heard that the movie is a wonderful movie. It is close to what we really went through.

(RTU - To date, Rachel has not seen "Schindler's List." The thought of going causes too much stress. I think we all can understand.)

Rachel continues:

And then, he gave me a plaque, a recognition, that I made tapes. That tape was played in high schools. He thanked me and sent me a personal letter in Omaha.

That was quite an experience, to meet such a giant man like Steven.

RTU:

What was your impression of him?

Rachel:

I thought that he was a humanitarian. He was a good man. He kinda felt the hurt with us.

RTU:

How do you know that?

Rachel:

I felt it. I saw it and I felt it. That he was a very very warm and wonderful person, to be able to make that movie. That's something else.

I am very sorry. Someone asked him the question what is the hardest in his life. He said it was the divorce. I am very sorry, Steven, that it happened to you.

I know now you are a happy man with children and grandchildren and I love you very much.

RTU:

Sounds like you connected with him?

Rachel:

Yeah.

RTU:

What did he say to you when you parted?

Rachel:

He gave me a little hug. He gave me a little kiss and he said, "I love you and good luck."

A Love Triangle - Rachel, Abe and Rivkah Sass

RTU:

Rachel, in your book, we have used an interview with your friend, Abe Sass.

I know that Abe Sass and his wife Rivkah were very important to you while they were living in Omaha. Can you tell us a little about that?

Rachel:

I met Rivkah and Abe at a Friday night dinner at their home. When I came in, I didn't know the people. The candles were lit.

Abe made Kiddush (blessing over the wine) with the tradition like I knew from home.

That impressed me so much that words could not tell. I stayed there and I had a nice Friday night dinner. He asked me who I was.

I told him I am a Holocaust survivor. I showed him my number (15254) on my arm.

He knew a lot about the Holocaust. So, he kinda felt for me. So, it was 10:00 p.m. and they took me home. I lived nearby.

Since then, Abe and Rivkah were my guiding light. I don't know how to say it. I loved them and they loved me.

They made me what I am today. We had wonderful years together.

I did not think a lot about me. I was a Holocaust survivor. I didn't go to college. I didn't go to high school. I said, "Abe and Rivkah, I don't have any diplomas like you have.

You are educated. Why would you want me to be your friend?" And Rivkah says to me, "Rachel, what you could do, any college doesn't teach. You are talented."

When I would cook for them, especially Abe, he loved it. I cooked in the old-fashioned way.

They are the most wonderful people. They helped me. I had breakfast with them all the time.

I was a volunteer at the hospital and Abe would cook breakfast for me every morning for 2 years. Abe made wonderful coffee.

RTU:

Rachel, Abe says you were a volunteer at a hospital and it gave you a great sense of satisfaction. Can you tell us about that?

Rachel:

I loved it. I was a tea lady. We would go into rooms and serve cookies, juice and coffee. There was very little tea.

It was a very good experience for me. I did this with pride for four years.

I also did a project where I built brassieres (padded) for ladies who lost their breasts. I got an award for that.

I did make little hats for newborn babies. They were the cutest hats I made. My love was the tea cart. I was there for four years.

They were good to me. They loved me. It was a lot of fun and I never missed working (her schedule).

(RTU – Abe Sass remembers Rachel being extremely proud and having a great sense of accomplishment being able to help people. She was Rachel the Tea Lady with not much tea.)

Rachel continues:

My memories of Rivkah and Abe are sweet and the best in my years. I love 'em and will love 'em for the rest of my life. They're great. I love you Abe and Rivkah.

RTU:

Rachel, Abe told me this story about you. One day, you drove over to Abe and Rivkah's house. You were on your way to the Jewish Community Center to swim as was your custom.

This day, you wore your bathrobe. Underneath, you were dressed in a swimming suit.

Abe and Rivkah remember that you proudly stuck your leg out and said, "Look, these are the legs of a young girl."

Do you remember that and what can you say about that?

Rachel (slightly smiling):

Yes. It's true. One day I put on my bathing suit and said, "I want to show my body." I told Abe and Rivkah, "Look at my legs."

(RTU – Rachel was about 83 years old at the time.)

Rachel continues:

Rivkah said she wished she had legs like mine.

I do have pretty legs. I had pretty legs. I don't know if I still have pretty legs. It's true. Look at them.

Abe and Rivkah remember everything. Is it okay to tell this?

RTU:

Yes, it's okay.

As I understand, Abe helped you with reading. He gave you instructions about how to deal with some of your concerns and fears.

Rachel:

That's right. One day he came in and said he was going to read me a story. He read me stories that I had never heard before.

Then he said, "Why don't you read?" My reading wasn't the best. They diagnosed me with a sixth-grade reading (level).

He taught me how to pause, how to use commas. He taught me how to read really good. Thank you, Abe.

RTU:

And, he helped you sometimes when you were fearful? Tell me about that.

Rachel:

Sometimes, I would not be happy. My memories from home would come back. He cheered me. He took me everyplace they went.

They introduced me to the beautiful people who they knew. Never in my life would I have met people like this on my own.

RTU:

You know, as I understand, it was Abe who got you to speak about the Holocaust. It was Abe, who first took you to a school. You didn't have a plan or a speech.

Rachel:

One day he says to me, "Rachel, we are gonna talk to a class of sixth graders." I said, "Abe, I cannot do that. I will not do that."

He said, "You come with me." He took me by the hand and we went to a school. There were what seemed like about a hundred children.

(RTU – Abe Sass remembers when first presented with the idea of speaking about her experiences, Rachel was extremely reluctant. Rachel felt she could not "give a speech."

Abe told her she did not have to give a speech. He asked her if she could answer questions. Rachel felt she could do that. Rachel immediately took to the question format and thrived.

From the hundreds of letters Rachel has received from the school children, they really love her and connect with her. I tell Rachel she is changing the world. It's true.)

Abe Sass' Eyewitness Poem - Rachel's First Teaching Excursion - "My Name is Rachel"

"My name is Rachel"

Fifty 8th grade students watched her.

She slowly pulled up her sleeve.

"You ever see this before?"

She pointed to the blue numbers

Stark against her arm.

If they were sleepy, they woke up.

"Now, you ask me about anything, anything you want"

Slowly the questions came,

A quiet stream.

She stepped closer
Her hands moving with her words.
The current increased.

She looked at them all
Calling on them, one-by-one.

Her eyes glistened.
Tears came.

Still, she went on.
White caps appeared.
The current swelled.

More hands went up.
She gathered strength.
The tears stopped.

She was determined.
She had stories to tell.

The questions were bolder.

She grew stronger.

"My little brother, they pulled him

From the barrel he was hiding in."

Eyes wide, total silence.

"They shot him, right there."

Much later, as the students left the room,

They came to her

One-by-one and embraced her.

When the door closed she looked at me.

"Nu, was I ok?"

"Yes, Rachel, much more than OK".

(End of Abe Sass' Poem - "My Name Is Rachel")

Rachel continues:

I talked to them. He (Abe) sat at the side. He said to me. "Rachel, on your grave it should be written, Rachel the teacher." It's true.

Rivkah and Abe took me into their lives. They made me strong. They helped me in my life. There are no words that I could say to thank them for it.

I miss them very much. There are no other people in the world like them.

RTU:

Why do you miss them?

Rachel:

They are humanitarians. They are wonderful people. I didn't have to call to come over. We made a garden together.

We had a lot of fun together. Sometimes me and Abe sat outside and Abe would read me a story.

It was the sweetest, most pleasant time in my life knowing Rivkah and Abe. I was part of their home.

Whenever they went out for big things, they included me. I asked them why they included me.

They said, "Rachel, you are part of us and we are comfortable to have you with us."

RTU:

And you knew they truly loved you.

Rachel:

Yes.

I said, "Maybe it's a little too much of me." They said, "No, when you come in, you come in with a light."

RTU:

The reason you miss them, I understand, is that they moved away.

Rachel:

They moved away from me. I was sick. I was in disbelief. They were hiding from me, because they knew it would hurt me. But then, I had to face the truth.

I love you (Abe and Rivkah) and I always will for the rest of my life.

My Biggest Hurt

Rachel:

My biggest hurt was my brother, Jacob. I can still see him walking away from me sixty years later. He is still calling my name. I haven't forgotten.

Abe:

It's a big hurt.

Rachel:

Yes, it is.

Abe:

When you have a hurt like that which is sooo... deep and you live past the Holocaust and come to America, are there times when it comes back to you even in the middle of your life here in America?

Rachel:

Yes. Yes it does. I am quiet. I just lay down. I cry a little bit. There is nothing else I can do.

Abe:

Just recently, you told me you have been going to a few schools and answering questions that kids have. Does that help the hurt at all?

Rachel:

Hmm... Not really. But it makes me feel good that the children listen to me. I don't know if they can comprehend; if they could feel.

Yes, it makes me feel good.

But that story has to be told. Yes and I feel good about it. I cry like I.. .. I didn't think my little brother would come out in the conversation, but it did.

Abe (softly):

Ah-hum. How do the kids react to you? Here you are going in. They are like sixth grade kids or something like that. What is it like?

Rachel:

They ask me questions. One little boy asked me. I told him that we slept in barracks, that there were 2000 people.

So he asked me, "Did you have a big window? Did you have fun?"

Abe:

You just recently started doing this. What made you decide to start going to talk with these kids?

Rachel:

A few years ago, I didn't think I could talk about it. I couldn't. But then as I... like today, I could have said no to you, because it hurts.

But I said, "Why not. I want to tell. I want to tell." It's okay. I learned how to accept this and tell people what really happened.

Abe:

Earlier, you said that when you were in the concentration camps, you never really talked about G-d. What is your thinking about G-d now?

Rachel:

Now, I'm to G-d. I don't know what happened, but I am. I talk to G-d. I am a little bit more religious than I used to be. I go Friday night to the synagogue. I enjoy.

On Saturdays, I go to the synagogue. I enjoy. Yes, you have to hang on to something.

Abe:

Ah-huh. What do you feel at this point? What are you really proudest of in your life? What gives you that feeling of pride?

Rachel:

Well, when I came to Omaha from Landsberg (Germany), I am proudest of myself; because without a home, without an identity, without a mother or father, without a relative, I had no one. We were free.

Abe:

If you were with a bunch of kids now, like those you talk to, and they asked you, "What kind of wisdom can you give us?

What kind of thing can you tell us based on what you went through?" And these kids were sitting there, what would you tell them?

Rachel:

I would tell them:

- Be good to your parents - number one.

- Go to school - number two.

- Make a trade or whatever you do in your life.

- Be honest.

- Save

- Work hard.

And then you'll make it. That's what I did. No one ever gave me anything. I had no one to help me; aunt, uncle to call, no mother, no father to help me, give me, didn't.

I had to help myself.

- And save money.

Abe:

Suppose one of those kids said to you, "I try to do all those things you mentioned. How do I get that feeling about the joy of life?

What should I do about that?" What would you tell him?

Rachel:

I would tell him, "Just do the right thing. Don't lie. Be honest and go on with your life. Do the best you can. But, honesty is the best. And work hard, you have to earn."

Abe:

If your parents were alive and saw that, would they be proud of you?

Rachel:

I think so. I do love life. I like the outdoors. I like the fresh air, my garden. That all makes 'em happy. I don't need a lot in my life to make me happy.

I never said, "You have more and I have less." I am happy with what I have in my life. I think I am the richest (person) there is. I don't need any more. I've got everything.

And I like to save.

Abe:

Wonderful.

Conclusion of the Abe Sass

Interview

Abe:

Your world changed sooo much from the time you were growing up until all of this horror started. How has that affected you in your life now?

Rachel:

You mean talking about after the war?

Abe:

Well, it seems to me that you have gone through a lot of horrible experiences during the war.

And, I guess in my mind, I am thinking that, in a way, I am going back to the time I was referring to in the beginning of our talk, when you were breathing that fresh air.

I was thinking. You know, if somebody goes through so much horror as you did, you still have that incredible spark to think how wonderful this world is.

Rachel:

To live, yes.

Abe:

Absolutely.

Rachel (emphatically):

Really.

Abe:

And so that world of yours, when you were growing up, changed so dramatically. I mean so, I mean a major big big change. How has that affected you?

Rachel (pause, crying):

Well....

Abe (softly):

Ah-hah

Rachel:

Talking about after the war?

Abe:

Talking about whatever you want. After the war, during the war, whatever you want.

Rachel:

Well, of course, we are hurt. But, life goes on. I didn't want to, but I was (hurt). When I came to this country, I was a 20-year-old.

I saw cars, people dressed, people having homes. I saw people live. You know, I said, "I don't want to live with my past. I want to see the light, instead of the dark."

"I want to make my life as happy, as successful, as I possibly can."

And this is what I did. And this is my aim, to feel good about life. I am hurt. But, I don't want to live with it. I want to live a normal life. Originally, I am not normal.

But, I try to live as normal as I possibly can. I pretend I am normal. I like clothes. I like money. I like a home. I like a car. I want to have this and I do."

Abe:

I remember one time you talked about having a house with a big window.

Rachel:

A big window and a car and a diamond or two, a fur coat and a few dollars in my pocketbook. We worked hard. We were both professionals, Carl and I.

Abe:

Did you have thoughts about what you wanted for your life while you were in the concentration camps? Did you have any of those kinds of thoughts?

Rachel:

No. When we were in Auschwitz or any camps, we never ever talked about G-d; that any of us, any, will live through the war.

Never. Ever. Ever. There was no tomorrow.

When we looked through the fields and saw people working in the fields, there were birds.

And there were people in cars. We looked at the sky. It was so beautiful and blue.

But, here we are in a death camp. We never knew who would live through. We never, ever, talked about that.

(We) never talked about that a miracle was going to happen. G-d? We never had G-d in our hearts. We never knew from holidays. All our lives we were afraid.

(End of the Abe Sass interview)

Rachel's Closing Remarks

RTU:

Rachel, what can you tell people about life based on your experience with hardship?

Rachel:

Well... life can be hard. Life can be beautiful. I choose to be as happy as I can be and enjoy no matter what you have. I was happy with it.

I was a free person. I enjoy freedom. I like the United States. They gave me the opportunity to be what I am. I had my own business. I was successful.

But, you have to be strong in order to help yourself and to do things you want to do and not wait until somebody else is going to help, somebody else is going to do it for you.

You gotta do it yourself.

RTU:

Rachel, for as long as I have known you, I have never seen you get really angry, what people would say ticked-off, to lose it.

I have never heard you curse. You always hold a certain amount of decorum or stability. Why do you think that is?

Rachel:

Well, that is my character. I appreciate everything I have, everything I accomplished. I never get angry at anyone. That's a good question.

But, this is the way I am. I see things in the better way. I never see the dark and the bitterness like some people have.

I'm happy whatever comes in life, the way life takes me and I never fail. I can't be angry at anyone.

I can sense, which person is a good person and which one is not. If they are not, I just leave them alone and don't criticize.

If somebody hurts me, I just walk away. I am quiet. I say, "It's one of those things. Tomorrow will be a better day."

RTU:

Rachel, how do you feel about the German people?

Rachel:

I feel that whatever the Nazi regime did, they should never be forgiven.

I cannot be mean or angry to a German just because the person is a German. That person is a person, a German person. But she is a person.

I cannot hurt her in any way. I cannot be mean or angry to them. I treat them like I would everyone else. I cannot hate them.

(RTU – Rachel and Carl employed a woman of German descent in their clothing store for almost 2 decades. Rachel remains friends with her.)

"This is my heart. I am not writing or reading anything.

I am a free person. I am me. I am happy. I enjoy little things, which make me happy.

With me, everything is good. Everything is sweet and beautiful."

Aftermath of the Holocaust
The Cover-Up

(April 12, 1945: Generals Eisenhower, Omar Bradley and George Patton inspecting the improvised crematory pyre at Ohrdruf forced labor camp.)

(RTU - As World War 2 was winding down, there was a concerted attempt by the Nazis to eliminate as much evidence of the Holocaust as possible.

However, there was not enough time for the Nazis to destroy the evidence. The scope of the horror was just too massive.

By 1945, General Eisenhower, Supreme Allied Commander, anticipated Holocaust deniers and detractors with the passage of time.

General Eisenhower believed there would be an attempt to re-characterize the crimes as propaganda and overstatement.

General Eisenhower stated:

"The same day I saw my first horror camp. It was near the town of Gotha.

I have never been able to describe my emotional reactions when I first came face-to-face with indisputable evidence of Nazi brutality and ruthless disregard of every shred of decency.

Up to that time I had known about it only generally or through secondary sources. I am certain however, that I have never at any time experienced an equal sense of shock.

I visited every nook and cranny of the camp because I felt it my duty to be in a position from then on to testify at first-hand about these things in case there ever grew up at home the belief or assumption that the stories of Nazi brutality were just propaganda.

Some members of the visiting party were unable to go through with the ordeal.

I not only did so but as soon as I returned to Patton's (another American General) headquarters that evening I sent communications to both Washington and London, urging the two governments to send instantly to Germany a random group of newspaper editors and representative groups from the national legislatures.

I felt that the evidence should be immediately placed before the American and the British publics in a fashion that would leave no room for cynical doubt."

- RTU - The first entry in the Insights chapter is from a denier or revisionist. -

(RTU - In order to further document the atrocities of the Holocaust, General Eisenhower ordered all military with media credentials to visit the camps and take photographs.

General Eisenhower ordered the German citizens of the nearby town of Gotha to visit and work in the camp.

Following their forced visits to the Ohrduf labor camp, the mayor of Gotha and his wife committed suicide by hanging.6)

Addendum - Polish Jewry
A Brief History

RTU:

Rachel, I was looking at a taped interview by Carl. In his interview, he said there were a lot of problems between the Jewish and Gentile communities in Poland before the War and even during the initial part of the German invasion.

Some Poles' discrimination and disdain for the Jews was not always hidden.

Carl said the Gentiles would use the slur, "The Jews killed Jesus Christ."

Carl describes a time immediately after the German invasion. Carl was an officer in the Polish army.

An incident arose in his unit when the Polish Jews and Gentiles faced off and pointed rifles at each other.

Carl remembers telling the Polish Gentiles if they didn't stop, they, the Jews, would shoot them at that moment.

Carl did not say what prompted the confrontation. Bloodshed was avoided at the last minute through the intervention of a superior officer.[7]

Did you ever encounter any problems in Wolanow?

Rachel:

No.

RTU:

Were you ever yelled at or cursed?

Rachel:

No... Well, there was this time. It was Easter for the Christians.

I was standing outside my father's butcher shop and some Gentiles were nearby. They were saying bad things about the Jews.

I don't remember what they were saying, but I was afraid.

We all knew that for the Easter season, all the Jews better be careful. Don't go out at night. Stay at home for a few days. I could hear the adults talking about this.

I think it got better when Easter was over.

I don't think we should talk about this.

RTU:

It's okay. It helps explain what was really going on at the time. The Holocaust was a difficult time for everyone.

We will keep this part in the book. It will be okay. People need to know.

Comments by RTU on Polish Jewish History

(My comments about the History of Jews in Poland are based on information taken from Virtual Jewish History Tour - Jewish Virtual Library – A Project of the American-Israeli Enterprise.)[8]

RTU - For over a thousand years prior to World War 2, there had been a strong Jewish presence in Poland.

There was never a consistent, reliable, safe status or region in Poland for the Jews.

Poland was weak and not completely independent until 1918. Parts of Poland were under different political jurisdictions at different times.

Laws and statues regarding the Jews in Poland could change overnight. Tolerance or discrimination depended on ever-shifting circumstances.

Over the last millennium, areas of Poland were ruled by different factions. The status of the Jews often depended on the ruling party's attitude toward the Jews.

During the two hundred years of the crusades, Jews were persecuted throughout Europe. Poland served as a relative haven for Jewish refugees.

As a result of the Mongol invasions of 1241, Poland lost much of its population. Jews were encouraged to settle and establish themselves in Poland.

There was no central authority strong enough to stop the Jews from coming into Poland.

German Jews brought with them a dialect of the German language that became Yiddish.

Under King Casimir the Great and others, the ruling authorities recognized the administrative skills of the Jews. The rulers put these Jewish skills to good use.

This was not an unusual practice at that time. Some governments would encourage settlement of outsiders with useful skills.

Today's military and para-military mercenaries are a examples of this policy.

Vikings were invited to settle and administer in Moscow. Other Vikings or Normans settled in the Mediterranean rim to administer and sometimes take charge.

The Southern part of Italy was a Norman fiefdom until the time of the late Renaissance.

Acquiring good administrators was a problem. It was difficult for rulers to find good help. The Polish Jewish community was better educated, proficient, skillful and savvy.

The Jews knew how to accumulate capital and had the skills to put it to good use. Sometimes the Jews would loan money to their sovereigns.

The Jews formed most of the early banking communities.

The Jews were connected beyond constantly shifting borders. The Jewish community had the language skills for international commerce and politics.

The Jews very much fit the bill for Polish rulers in the 13th century and for many centuries thereafter.

However, unlike so many other places with skillful sub-communities, the Jewish political faction did not use its considerable skills to take over and rule Poland.

The Jews were not a warring faction within Poland. The Jews would defend their rulers and territory when allowed by the Polish ruling elite.

The Jews in Poland were often given protected status by the ruler. Often, it was necessary.

Because the Jews were skilled in language and had cross-border connections, they were desired for their ability to stimulate commerce, banking and international trade.

But what could be given could also be taken away. With the passage of time, the pendulum of favor could swing back in the direction of disfavor and the problems that came with it.

During the time of the guilds, the Jews in Poland were largely excluded because of the guild's monopolistic policies.

The Jews remained outside the guilds, but could pay exorbitant prices in order to compete against the guilds to a limited extent.

The Jews were blamed for the Black Death in the 15th century. Some towns began to block the Jews from residing within the cities.

In 1918, Poland became a sovereign state with defined borders.

At that time, many Jews were massacred. Some Poles believed the Jews were connected to Russian communism through a founder of Communism, Leon Trotsky. Trotsky was Jewish.

A tenet of Russian communism is the belief that we would all be better off if the Russians took complete control of the world.

For the Poles, communism meant the Russians were coming again to dominate Poland. The Russians controlled Poland for more than 40 years after World War 2.

The Jews had no particular status under communism. Marxism is atheistic.

At the start of World War 2, the Polish Jews were immediately persecuted. Many Jews had to display a Star of David. Rachel said she did not wear a star nor did other Jews in Wolanow.

Rachel emphatically believed that no Pole would hide a Jew.

Access to cash and bank accounts was immediately restricted as was the ability to work in certain industries.

These actions took place immediately after the German invasion.

In the beginning of the book, there is a chapter entitled: What Did Rachel Lose? -"From Milk and Honey" Childhood – Idyllic Village - Beautiful Family.

I added these closing comments about Jewish history in Poland to help frame the complex social and political environment surrounding any Jew in Poland at the time of the Holocaust.

In Poland, discrimination against the Jews was not new.

You know the rest of the story from Rachel's perspective.

Could Rachel be a Leading Lady?
Rachel's Leading Lady Persona

I was drawn to Rachel Rosenberg by her reputation. You know how it is. Every once-in-a-while you hear of someone "You just have to meet."

Many times it is just hyperbole.

In the case of Rachel Rosenberg, I kept hearing her name and references to her remarkable story. I started to take note.

In time, I was hooked and wanted to meet this women in order to find out for myself.

I particularly wanted to know if she harbored anger, guilt or resentment toward the world or any groups, persons, etc. How had she adjusted? I had no idea what I would find.

To my surprise, from the moment I met Rachel in her kitchen, I was taken with her vivacity, kindness, openness and love.

At the time of my first meeting with Rachel, she was caring for her husband Carl who was in cognitive decline from Alzheimer's Dementia.

From my medical background, I had come to believe you can tell a lot about a person when they care for someone with demanding medical issues.

Rachel's devotion to Carl was truly remarkable. She was not just doing the best she could. Rather, she lovingly saw to his needs.

She did not abuse, dismiss or disrespect him in any way. Rachel did not refer to his condition as a barrier. She had overcome the barrier.

The bond between Rachel and Carl was deep. I still remember that day and my first impression of Rachel.

Someone asked me to discuss the most outstanding characteristic that I found in my relationship with Rachel Rosenberg.

Rachel's Leading Lady Persona

I have studied human interaction and attraction. I must admit that I can't figure Rachel out. I told her she is definitely a "leading lady."

A leading lady is a woman who gains the attention of everyone in the room.

She may or may not be the smartest, most-beautiful, most famous, best-dressed or any of that.

A leading lady draws homage from most if not all those present, men and women alike. She may not be seeking attention, yet, people are mysteriously drawn to her.

Men are especially drawn to leading ladies. Rachel remembers when she was young, people wanted to touch her. She didn't know what to do or why it was happening.

This touching phenomenon still occurs. People want to hug and kiss her. A leading lady does not demand attention, she gets the attention.

That is what qualifies Rachel or any other woman to be a leading lady. Rachel makes people feel good when they are around her.

I refer to this interaction as social resonance.

Many times I have found myself in a room full of people and Rachel. One after another, the men would come up and interact with her.

Men of all ages will come to her and have meaningful interactions. It is remarkable and predictable.

Let me give you an example. I had occasion to be in Rachel's home. The doorbell rang and there was a young man with two children.

The man said, "Hi Rachel. I'm ____. I don't know if you remember me. I sat beside you on a plane when we were travelling together.

That was 12 years ago. I told you I would visit you someday and here I am."

I can remember my immediate reaction very vividly. "Who does that? Why is this happening? What about Rachel could draw someone like this?"

I have accused her of emitting some chemical into the air, perhaps a mysterious pheromone (attraction hormone).

I could say more about Rachel. But this is really her story. I know you have heard it before in respect to others, but in the deepest sense of the expression:

EVERYONE LOVES RACHEL.

Allow me to use one of Rachel's favorite expressions from the book.

"It's true."

Post Script:

RTU - Several years ago, I heard Zev Kedem, one of the youngest Holocaust survivors, discuss his experience in the Auschwitz Concentration Camp.

What struck me about Zev Kedem's story were his 3 most important strategies for survival in the camps. They represented things he could do for himself in that horrible set of circumstances.

I found these survival characteristics very much at work in Rachel's experience. They are –

1. You had to be hidden, more than when they first came for you. You should not stick out or call unnecessary attent ion to yourself.

Rachel relates how she tried very hard not to call attention to herself. She stayed away from the Germans.

Prisoners with something to say could be heard and punished.

Rachel found herself listening closely but saying very little, even to her fellow prisoners. "I kept my mouth shut. I did what I was told."

2. You had to be clever. Try to figure out what is or will be going on and take advantage of it to the best of your ability.

Sometimes you had to go it alone and not listen to others.

Rachel learned where things were in the camps and occasionally took advantage of it. She made stockings for her brother Jacob from the clothing barracks.

3. You had to be skillful. Make yourself useful.

"Essential worker" was the term in the movie, "Schindler's List."

Stand out only when it came to demonstrating your value to the Nazis.

If it was work the Nazis valued, become good at it. Better yet, become the best at it.

Rachel became a top seamstress. The Nazis gave her accolades on more than one occasion. This had to have helped.

Final Thoughts

Rachel and I were discussing Carl's two brothers. Both died in Auschwitz as we related in the book.

Rachel said both brothers were strong-willed and restless. This led to their deaths.

Then Rachel said to me, "Tom, you wouldn't have made it. You are too strong-willed. You would have done something and it would have got you killed.

Anything out of the ordinary was enough to have you taken out and killed. You wouldn't have taken it."

I have thought a lot about Rachel's comment. I think she was right about me.

What about you, Dear Reader, could you have "taken it?"

Could you have survived?

Bye - Help Rachel Get Her Story Out

P.S. – Would you consider leaving me a review on Amazon.com? It would help and encourage me. Don't forget.

Thanks,

Rachel

Visit Our Website

www.theholocaustscream.com

Leave me a comment. I would like to know how people feel about my story

(Rachel Rosenberg and Robert Urban)

Bibliography

1. Cover image - The Burning Piece of Cardboard and Ashes. Copyright Sachabert @ Dreamstine I.D. 22203029.

Royalty free with license to use January 2013

2. Rachel Rosenberg. (n.d.). Personal photograph.

3. Robert Urban. (2103). Personal photograph.

4. High definition bird image. (n.d.). Public Domain Images. [Photo].

Retrieved November 2012 from http://www.public-domain-image.com/fauna-animals-public-domain-images-pictures/birds-public-domain-images-pictures/page/15/

5. Vin'y, Arielle. (2010). Being a Bird. [Poem]. Cleveland, Ohio.

6. Urban, Robert. (2012, September 8). "Jewish Holocaust Camps Survivor Addresses The Issue - The Holocaust Did Not Happen".

YouTube. [Video].

Retrieved September 9, 2012
from http://www.youtube.com/
watch?v=LsQeWoas_LQ&feature=youtu.be

7. Moishe Boiman, Rachel's Father. (n.d.). Personal photograph.

8. St. Louis Captain Gustav Schroeder negotiates landing permits for the passengers with Belgian officials in the port of Antwerp.

(1939). Antwerp, Belgium. [Photo].

United States Holocaust Memorial Museum, courtesy of Betty Troper Yaeger.

Retrieved November 24, 2012 from

http://digitalassets.ushmm.org/photoarchives/
detail.aspx?id=27075

9. Close-up of an Angry German Shepherd Dog. (n.d.). Public Domain Images.

[Photo]. Retrieved November 15, 2012 from

https://www.google.com/search?q=public+dom
ain+images+german+shepherd&hl=en&tbo=u&t
bm=isch&source=univ&sa=X&ei=G8DIUI3FA6e
r2AW2oYCgDA&sqi=2&ved=0CDUQsAQ&biw=1
180&bih=825

10. SS collar patches of the Second World War. (2010, September).

National Archives and Records Administration. [Photo].

Retrieved November 22, 2012 from http://en.wikipedia.org/wiki/ File:Kragenpatten,_13._SS-TK-Standarte.jpg

11. Establishing racial descent by measuring an ear at the Kaiser Wilhelm Institute for Anthropology, Germany.

(n.d.). National Archives and Records Administration, College Park, Md. [Photo]. Retrieved November 5, 2012 from

http://www.ushmm.org/outreach/en/media_ph. php?ModuleId=10007679&MediaId=4227

12. Koehl, Robert Lewis. (1989). The SS: A History 1919–1945. Tempus Publishing Limited ISBN 0-7524-2559-5.

13. Dorsm365. Detail of the main gate at Dachau concentration camp in Germany, displaying the infamous "Arbeit Macht Frei" slogan. (2007, January). Wikimedia Commons. [Photo].

Retrieved November 15, 2012 from http://en.wikipedia.org/wiki/File:Arbeit_Macht _Frei_Dachau_8235.jpg

14. Rachel Rosenberg's Arm Tattoo. (n.d.). Personal photograph.

15. Peter Hellman, Lili Meier, Beate Klarsfeld (eds). (1981). Franz Hossler's paraphrased

speech. *The Auschwitz Album*, Random House, New York, ISBN 394-51932-9 p. 166

16. An Historic Photographic Documentation of the Extermination Process at Auschwitz-Birkenau. (n.d). Holocaust Survivors and Remembrance Project: "Forget You Not"™.

[Photo]. Retrieved November 3, 2012 from http://isurvived.org/AUSCHWITZ_TheCamp.html

17. Josef Mengele, German physician and SS captain. (n.d.). National Museum of Auschwitz-Birkenau. [Photo]. Retrieved November 15, 2012 from http://www.ushmm.org/wlc/en/media_ph.php?ModuleId=10007060&MediaId=2653

18. Rosenberg, Carl. (n.d.). Omaha World Herald. [Interview]. As accounted for by Rachel Rosenberg.

19. Josef Mengele. (n.d.). United States Holocaust Memorial Museum, Washington, DC.

Retrieved September 30, 2012 from http://www.ushmm.org/wlc/en/article.php?ModuleId=10007060

20. Crematorium 5. (n.d.). Auschwitz Concentration Camp: The Gas Chambers & Crematoria - Mass Extermination.

[Photo]. Holocaust Research Project: Holocaust Education & Archive Research Team. Retrieved November 22, 2012 from http://www.holocaustresearchproject.org/o thercamps/auschwitzgaschambers.html

21. Matti8482. (2011, April 19). "SS-Aufseherin: Female Camp Guards 1938-1945.". YouTube. [Video, 1:12]. Retrieved October 9, 2012 from http://www.youtube.com/ watch?v=W6Hiy dokKdE

22. He Ain't Heavy. (2013). Robert Urban personal collection.

23. Jakob Vann (2010). Jacob Vann's Bar Mitzvah tribute to Rachel's brother Jacob Boiman.

24. JoJan. (2007, May 20). Original boxcar used for transports to the Nazi concentration camps; Fort van Breendonk, Belgium. Auschwitz concentration camp. WikiCommons.

[Photo]. Retrieved October 23, 2012 from http://en.wikipedia.org/wiki/Auschwitz_concen tration_camp

25. Tatiana. (2011, May 6). Dove. Clker.com. [Photo]. Retrieved November 11, 2012 from http://www.clker.com/clipart-122757.html

26. Potatoes. (2005, January 21). United States Department of Agriculture. Potatoes. Wikipedia. [Photo].

Retrieved November 8, 2012 from
http://en.wikipedia.org/wiki/File:Potatoes.jpg

27. Carl Rosenberg. (n.d.). Personal

photograph.

28. Carl Rosenberg. (n.d.). Personal

photograph.

29. Rachel and Morris Rosenberg. (1950). Personal photograph.

30. Eisenhower, Dwight D. Gen. (1945, April 15). Letter, General Eisenhower to General Marshall concerning his visit to a Germany internment camp near Gotha (Ohrdruf), April 15, 1945

[Dwight D. Eisenhower's Pre-Presidential Papers, Principal File, Box 80, Marshall George C. (6)].

The Dwight D. Eisenhower Presidential Library and Museum, part of the Presidential Libraries System administered by the National Archives and Records Administration.

Retrieved November 26, 2012 from

http://www.eisenhower.archives.gov/research/o nline_documents/holocaust/1945_04_15_DDE _to_Marshall.pdf

31. Rosenberg family. (n.d.). Personal photograph.

32. Sass, Abe. (n.d.). "My Name is Rachel" - An Eyewitness Poem About Rachel's First Teaching Excursion, [Poem]. Omaha, Nebraska.

33. General Dwight D. Eisenhower (third from left) views the charred remains of inmates of the Ohrdruf camp. (1945, April 12). Ohrdruf, Germany.

National Archives and Records Administration, College Park, Md. [Photo]. Retrieved November 5, 2012 from

http://www.ushmm.org/wlc/en/media_ph.php?MediaId=3720

34. "Ike and the Death Camps." (2004). Dwight D. Eisenhower Memorial Commission. Retrieved November 15, 2012 from http://www.eisenhowermemorial.org/ stories/death-camps.htm

35. Rosenberg, Carl. (1988). National Public Radio. [Interview]. As accounted for by Rachel Rosenberg.

36. The Holocaust. (n.d.) Jewish Virtual Library.Retrieved September 27, 2012 from

http://www.jewishvirtuallibrary.org/jsource/vjw/Poland.html

37. Rachel Rosenberg and Robert Urban. (January, 2013) Personal photograph of James Steele used with permission.

38. Auschwitz Camp Plans. (n.d.) Wikepedia Commons

39. He Ain't Heavy....From - The Hollies by B.Scott and B. Russell. Idielyrics http://www.oldielyrics.com/lyrics/the_ho llies/he_aint_heavy_hes_my_brother.html

40. File. (August 2007) The StoryCorps Archive in the American Folklife Center at the Library of Congress.

Notes

1. Photo 1. (Page 10). Personal photograph of Rachel Rosenberg.

2. Photo 2. (Page 14) Personal photograph of Robert Urban

3. Photo 3. (Page 15). Picture of a Gull. This file (High definition bird images) is in <u>public domain</u>, not copyrighted, no rights reserved, free for any use.

You can use this picture: High definition bird images for any use including commercial purposes without the prior written permission and without fee or obligation.

4. Poem 1. (Page 15-16). "Being a Bird", by Arielle Vin'y – (Rachel's Grandniece). Used with permission.

5. Video. (Page 18). Jewish Holocaust Camps Survivor Addresses The Issue - The Holocaust Did Not Happen.

6. Photo 4. (Page 20). Personal photograph of Moishe Boiman, Rachel's Father.

7. Photo 5. (Page 50). S.S. St. Louis Captain Gustav Schroder negotiating landing permits for the refugees at Antwerp, Belgium docks. Cop-

yright: United States Holocaust Memorial Museum.

8. Photo 6. (Page 56). Close-up of an angry German shepherd dog. This file (html code lists this as public domain) is in <u>public domain</u>, not copyrighted, no rights reserved, free for any use.

You can use this picture: High definition bird images for any use including commercial purposes without the prior written permission and without fee or obligation.

9. Photo 7. (Page 57). Nazi Death Head Collar Lapel (SS collar patches of the Second World War). Public image on file at the National Archives & Records Administration, College Park, Maryland showing SS insignia.

10. Photo 8. (Page 66). Establishing racial descent by measuring an ear at the Kaiser Wilhelm Institute for Anthropology, Germany. Copyright © United States Holocaust Memorial Museum, Washington, D.C.

11. Reference. (Page 51-52). Comment about racial purity. Library of Congress Military Legal Resources: Office of the United States Chief of Counsel for Prosecution of Axis Criminality, Nazi Conspiracy and Aggression.

12. Photo 9. (Page 71). Detail of the main gate at Dachau concentration camp in Germany, displaying the famous "Arbeit Macht Frei" slogan.

13. Photo 10 et al. – (Pages 72 – 112 – 124 - 125). Personal photograph of Rachel Rosenberg's Arm Tattoo, husband Carl and family et al.

14. Reference. (Page 72). Franz Hossler's paraphrased speech. Random House, New York, 1981, ISBN 394-51932-9

15. Photo 11. (Page 80). An Historic Photographic Documentation of the Extermination Process at Auschwitz-Birkenau.

Photo credit: Holocaust Survivors and Remembrance Project: "Forget You Not"™.

16. Photo 13. (Page 76). Josef Mengele, German physician and SS captain. Copyright © United States Holocaust Memorial Museum, Washington, DC

17. Reference. (Page 59). Carl Rosenberg interview. Omaha World Herald, n.d. First-hand account from Rachel Rosenberg.

18. Reference. (Page 59). Josef Mengele. Copyright © United States Holocaust Memorial Museum, Washington, DC

19. Photo 14. (Page 80). Crematorium 5. Copyright SJ H.E.A.R.T 2007.

20. Photo 15. (Page 82). SS-Aufseherin: Female Camp Guards 1938-1945. Standard YouTube License.

21. Photo 16. 17. 18. (Page 88-103-195). He Ain't Heavy, He's My Brother et al.

Personal photographs of Robert Urban

22. Bar Miztvah Address (Page 88) - Jacob Vann's Loving Tribute to Rachel's Brother Jacob Boiman. Used with permission

23. Photo 17. (2013). (Page 196) James Steele – personal photograph

24. Auschwitz Camp Plans (n.d.) (Page 111) Wikepedia Commons.

25. He Ain't Heavy....From - The Hollies by B.Scott and B. Russell. Idielyrics http://www.oldielyrics.com/lyrics/the_hollies/he_aint_heavy_hes_my_brother.html

Addendum:

A. Cover image - The Burning Piece of Cardboard and Ashes. Copyright Sachabert @ Dreamstine I.D. 22203029. Royalty free with license to use January 2013.

Insights

RTU: Detractors and deniers.

1. It is hard to believe that in the face of all that incriminating evidence and the living testimony of Rachel Rosenberg and many other victims, there are still Holocaust detractors and deniers.

Where did the 6 million people go?

What form does denial and propaganda take? How about an example? Check it out for yourself and from Germany: <u>Deniers, propagandists and revisionists</u>

Do these so-called free speech comments belong in Rachel's book. Definitely, we will encounter them. Only now, we are prepared, thanks to Rachel and all the others who keep the Holocaust alive.

Please don't send me other examples.

RTU: Animal confinement facilities?

2. On January 27, 2013, I attended a presentation by Professor Paul Jaskot about the architecture of Auschwitz. What struck me were the aerial views of Auschwitz CC.

Professor Jaskot stated that the Nazis were constantly re-shaping the Auschwitz Camp. Rachel
was caught up in this building when she had to
carry the 75 pound blocks.

The plan resembles the efficient organized plans
of animal confinement facilities. Rachel said she
and the others in her barracks were like lambs
being led to the slaughter.

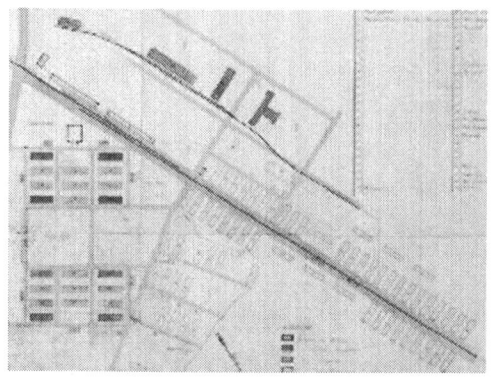

(Auschwitz Camp plans resembling animal confinement facilities)

This indicates the disconnect between the hu-
manity of the Master Race versus its victims. The
inmates were to be used and processed as effi-
ciently as possible for the good of the Third
Reich.

Others were discarded. Sometimes immediately
which was the case with Rachel's mom and her
brother, Motel.

Rachel and the others were seen by the Nazi in a
way humans see confined animals. The Nazis

could look Rachel in the eye because they considered her kind to be sub-human.

The plans also resemble a modern circuit board for the moving of electrons.

You're theholocaustscream.com insight will go here.

To submit a customer review: You need to use an Amazon account that has been charged for the purpose of a physical or digital item. Free digital downloads don't qualify.

You don't need to have purchased the product you're reviewing. There's a 48-hour waiting period after your first physical order has been completely shipped, or your digital item has been purchased, before you will be able to submit your review.

Remember to please give us a review.

Insight from Brooke – "this book is horrifying. its one of those books that you just can't put down. i feel deeply connected to this story as sympothy just pours out of me. if only we could go back in time and change this terrible part of history."

From Susan – "Best and easiest book to read. The way you constructed it was so unique!"

From Ronald B. - If it were not for survivors like Rachel then I would never know what my parents and their siblings went through. You see I am very angry that my mother was in three camps but has not said one word to her children.

From Talia Z. – I would say this generation (grandchildren of survivors) is definitely affected as well. Maybe not 100% but definitely affected. -

Submit an Amazon.com review for digital and physical books.

Get future video developments – Subscribe to our YouTube channel at:

YouTube.com/user/holocaustshoah1939.

You do not have to have a YouTube account to subscribe to our channel. Check the subscribe button to the right of the channel title. New video notifications will be sent to you by email. Easy.

38433095R00121

Made in the USA
Lexington, KY
09 January 2015